Cost-Ef
Home Building

A Design
and Construction
Handbook

NAHB Research Center

HOME
BUILDER
PRESS

Home Builder Press®
National Association of Home Builders

In some cases, this handbook names specific products offered by certain manufacturers. The intent is solely to help explain the type of material represented by the products. Reference to these products does not constitute an endorsement by the National Association of Home Builders (NAHB) nor the NAHB Research Center (Research Center). This handbook also includes many tables from various sources that are intended as guidelines. The NAHB and the Research Center are not responsible for the accuracy of these tables. Where necessary, the original sources for the tables or a qualified engineer should be consulted to verify design information. Finally, the techniques presented in this handbook have not necessarily been accepted in all local or national building codes at this time. Before using these techniques, a builder should check to be sure that they comply with the local building code. The NAHB and the Research Center are not responsible for any construction that violates any building code.

Cost-Effective Home Building: A Design and Construction Handbook
ISBN 0-86718-391-8

Library of Congress Cataloging-in-Publication Data

Waite, Timothy J.
    Cost-effective home building : a design and construction handbook
/ NAHB Research Center ; [principal author, Timothy J. Waite].
        p. cm.
    Rev. ed. of: Reducing home building costs with optimum value engineered
design and construction / NAHB Research Center. 1977.
    ISBN 0-86718-391-8
    1. House construction. 2. House construction—Cost effectiveness.
I. NAHB Research Center. II. NAHB Research Center. Reducing home building
costs with optimum value engineered design and construction.
III. Title.
TH4812.W34 1994
690'.8—dc20   93-39104
                                                                   CIP

Copyright © 1994 by the
National Association of Home Builders of the United States
1201 15th Street, N.W.
Washington, DC 20005

All rights reserved. No part of this book may be reproduced or used in any form or by any means, electronic or mechanical, including photocopying and recording, or by any information storage and retrieval system without permission in writing from the publisher.

For further information, please contact:

NAHB Bookstore
1201 15th Street, N.W.
Washington, DC 20005
(800) 223-2665

1/94 HBP/VICTOR 2M

ACKNOWLEDGMENTS

We wish to recognize the National Association of Home Builders (NAHB) Research Committee, whose support made possible this new updated and expanded edition of the original publication, *Reducing Home Building Costs with OVE Design and Construction.*

Appreciation is also extended to the manufacturers and organizations that supplied information in the form of either text or tables for this handbook. Without this information, this work would not be complete. We particularly acknowledge the American Forest & Paper Association, the Wood Truss Council of America, the American Plywood Association, and the American Iron and Steel Institute for the information and assistance they provided. While acknowledging the assistance of these organizations, we wish to emphasize that this in no way implies their endorsement of the contents of this handbook.

The preparation of this handbook also required the talents of many dedicated professionals. The principal author of this publication is Timothy J. Waite, P.E., with review by Donald F. Luebs, author of the original "OVE Manual." Eric M. Lund provided the graphics and illustrations. Special thanks to Carol E. Soble for editing, and Heather H. Fanning, Maria M. Gilmore, and June M. Prescop for work on the text and formatting.

CONTENTS

LIST OF TABLES

LIST OF FIGURES

PREFACE

With the publication of this handbook, we are facing the turn of the century and the uncertainty of tomorrow. The sharp rise in the price of lumber and the new limitations on tree harvesting in the American Northwest make it imperative that we develop methods of using our resources more efficiently in the production of housing.

This handbook describes cost-effective techniques for designing and building homes. These techniques provide a practical means of reducing home building costs by using available building materials, labor skills, tools, and equipment. While these cost-reducing techniques are based on conventional wood-frame construction, the handbook also contains sections on engineered wood products and steel framing, which offer alternatives for the future.

With the federal government's transition to the metric system, it is foreseeable that the metric system will be the standard of measurement in this country within the next few years. With this in mind, soft metric conversions have been provided in the text and tables, not to set the standard for metric conversions but rather to promote familiarity with the metric system in preparation for the conversion.

While we have attempted to provide a generic handbook to cover most types of design conditions, it was beyond the scope to include design procedures and tables to cover high wind areas and Seismic Zones 3 and 4. If a structure is to be built in these areas, additional guidance will be necessary from the local building department and from a qualified professional.

Some of the techniques contained in this manual may differ from existing local building codes. In those instances, we urge local authorities to give the techniques careful consideration as a means of reducing building costs, increasing housing production, and conserving natural resources so that the nation's families may be better housed.

CHAPTER 1
INTRODUCTION

PURPOSE

The purpose of this handbook is to present cost-effective methods for home building based on familiar and available building materials and labor skills. The handbook outlines a series of practical design and construction techniques that contribute to the production of safe, durable, and economical homes.

The purpose of the handbook is consistent with the goals of the U.S. Department of Housing and Urban Development (HUD), which is concerned with increasing housing production and reducing costs to make better housing more accessible to the people of our nation. Application of the basic planning, engineering, and construction techniques described in this handbook where they are not currently used can produce a significant reduction in labor and material costs compared to many "conventional" practices. Ultimately, these cost savings will be passed on to the home buyer or renter.

This handbook is intended for use by designers, architects, engineers, builders, and subcontractors as well as by code officials, mortgage lenders, and others concerned with the safe and efficient production of housing.

COST-EFFECTIVE HOME BUILDING

Many cost-effective design and construction techniques have been developed over the years. While many of these techniques have become common practice in residential construction, many others are still not widely practiced either due to the resistance to change or a lack of information.

Cost-effective home building requires comparing alternative materials and methods to determine the least costly combinations that will result in the desired product. This is the approach that was originally known as Optimum Value Engineered (OVE) design and construction as introduced in the 1970s.

When home builders select house designs, materials, and products that represent the least costly combination, they are practicing a basic form of cost-effective home building. The cost-effective home building concept presented in this handbook expands on this practice by providing a systematic approach to selecting from a wide variety of cost-reducing techniques that cover each step of the design and construction process.

The cost-reducing techniques presented are intended to be compatible with wood-frame construction, which represents most of the housing built in the United States today. Although traditional wood-frame construction is inherently an efficient process, the techniques presented in this handbook use available materials and labor skills even more efficiently. The labor force will not need to be retrained in basic skills; however, workers may need to be instructed in applying these skills to ensure the cost-effective use of time and materials.

Although the details in this handbook are presented in terms of single-family homes, most of the techniques also apply to other light-frame housing types such as duplexes, townhouses, and low-rise (garden) apartments. In addition, most cost-effective concepts are adaptable to on-site, panelized, or modular building methods. The advantages of cost-effective home building described in this handbook can be applied to houses in all price ranges and of all architectural styles without sacrificing the essential quality of construction. However, the most significant savings are realized in more affordable housing where a savings of several thousand dollars may enable a first-time home buyer to obtain a mortgage.

Designers and builders will find a wide variety of cost-reducing ideas to choose from. The concepts are not simply a collection of unrelated cost-saving methods but rather a series of planning, engineering, and construction techniques that can work together. Although it may not be possible to employ all of these cost-effective building techniques, each one can contribute to reducing the cost of a home.

BACKGROUND

This handbook is an updated and expanded version of the "OVE Manual" published in 1977. The original OVE Manual was produced by the NAHB Research Center (Research Center) under the sponsorship of HUD and was entitled *Reducing Home Building Costs with Optimum Value Engineered Design and Construction.*[1] This manual was widely distributed across the country.

The original OVE concept was based on conventional wood-frame construction that used a 2-foot (610 mm) planning module for better material usage. All framing members were spaced 24 inches (610 mm) on center for structural continuity and simplicity. A prototype house was built to demonstrate the OVE system. Building code approvals were obtained for the house under the performance provisions of the local building code on the basis of engineering and full-scale test results. Time and method studies were conducted by the Research Center engineering staff during construction to determine labor and material requirements.

---

[1]Optimum Value Engineered Building System, Contract No. H-1315, U.S. Department of Housing and Urban Development, January 1973. The Optimum Value Engineered building system was originally developed by the NAHB Research Center, Inc., through a contract from the Department of Housing and Urban Development under Operation BREAKTHROUGH, type B programs.

Labor and material requirements for a conventional house of similar size were then determined and compared with those of the OVE prototype house. Cost determinations for both the conventional and OVE houses were based on the direct labor and materials required to construct the houses. The OVE house achieved a total direct cost savings of more than 12 percent. Of this, 69 percent was in material and 31 percent in labor. Framing and related items such as sheathing and siding accounted for the largest major category of savings, representing 65 percent of the total labor and material savings. This was followed by foundation savings—13 percent; mechanical systems—11 percent; and other—11 percent. The "other" category included such items as interior trim and paint. These savings are shown in Figure 1.1.

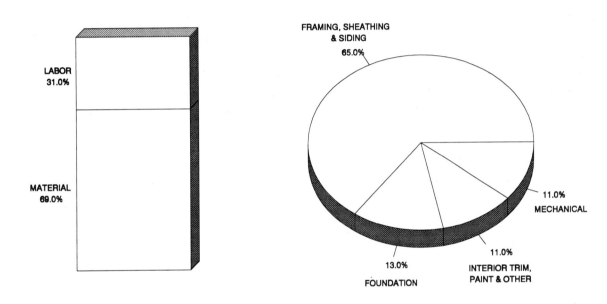

**FIGURE 1.1 Distribution of 12 Percent Direct Cost Savings
Achieved with Cost-Effective Design and Construction**

REDUCING HOME BUILDINGS COSTS TODAY

While the concepts and techniques presented in the original OVE Manual are still valid today, several changes have taken place in the industry. In 1991, as the result of an extensive testing program conducted by the lumber industry in cooperation with the U.S. Forest Products Laboratory, lumber design values were revised. With these new values, the strength and span tables for each species, class, and size were changed, effectively outdating the tables in the OVE manual.

In addition, since the 1970s, the amount of timber available for harvesting from national forest lands has declined sharply as environmental concerns complicated the timber industry. Coupled with the resulting sharp increases in lumber prices, attention is now focused on cost-effective ways of using wood products in residential construction. The need for cost-effective home building is at least as relevant today as it was in the 1970s.

Consequently, the text, tables, and graphics in this "new and improved" handbook have been updated so that designers, builders, and others involved in home building can make use of current information. The text has been expanded to include a broader range of design and construction options, as well as the latest technologies such as alternatives to lumber and plywood and frost-protected shallow foundations. Metric conversions have also been included to be consistent with new federal government regulations.

METRIC CONVERSIONS

The Metric Conversion Act of 1975, as amended by the *Omnibus Trade and Competitiveness Act of 1988*, establishes the modern metric system (System International or SI) as the preferred system of measurement by the United States Federal Government. It also requires that the metric system be used in all federal procurements, grants, and business-related activities by September 30, 1992.[1] In addition, Executive Order 12770 (July 25, 1991), *Metric Usage in Federal Government Programs*, mandates each federal agency to make a transition to the use of metric units in government publications as they are revised on normal schedules.

With the federal government's transition to metric, it is foreseeable that the metric system will be the standard of measurement in this country within the next few years. With this in mind, soft (unrounded) metric conversions have been provided in the text and tables of this handbook, not to set the standard for metric conversions but rather to promote familiarity with the metric system in preparation for the conversion. However, the reader should be aware that many of these soft conversions may never be used.

Hard conversions (converting inch-pound measurements into rounded-off metric measurements) have been proposed for building construction. The result is slightly different material sizes and stud spacings. For example, Appendix A provides a list of proposed hard conversions for building materials and systems developed by the National Institute of Building Sciences (NIBS). While hard conversions provide easy-to-use metric values, they cannot be used until the metric-sized materials are commercially available.

As a step in the eventual transition to metric, this handbook includes soft metric conversions as follows:

1. Measurements in text or figures are given first in the inch-pound system and then, in parentheses, the number is converted into a soft metric measurement.

2. Most tables provide measurements first in the inch-pound system, then in a soft metric conversion. In other tables, where the addition of conversions would make the tables difficult to read, the soft metric conversions are provided in a following table.

---

[1]Metric Guide for Federal Construction, First Edition. The Construction Subcommittee of the Metrication Operating Committee of the Interagency Council for Metric Policy, National Institute of Building Sciences, Washington, DC.

3.   Traditional sizes of lumber such as the 2x4 or 2x6 are designated as such without conversions in the text.

BUILDING CODE ACCEPTANCE

Although many of the cost-effective techniques cited in this handbook are now recognized in major building codes, it is understandable that some local building codes or individual inspectors may not allow certain techniques to be used. Builders should check with local officials before using any new method or material that might not be recognized in the local code. However, the fact that a particular material or method is not recognized in the code does not necessarily preclude its use. Building officials in any jurisdiction have the option to allow an alternative material or method if they determine that it meets the intent of the code to safeguard the public health and safety. Builders or other potential users should actively pursue this option by meeting with the official and explaining their request.

CHAPTER 2
PLANNING AND DESIGN

MODULAR FRAMING PLANS

Cost-effective home building begins at the planning stage. To make home building cost-effective, the house should be designed around existing material sizes. This reduces the amount of cutoffs and waste material and results in optimal material usage.

The planning process begins with the structural members themselves. The structural members from foundation to roof should be spaced at the same modular dimension to facilitate construction for the framers, transfer loads directly through the supporting members to the foundation, and reduce the amount of material to be used. All structural members should be checked to ensure that they are not over- or underdesigned to support the design loads.

In many cases, the most cost-effective spacing for structural members, i.e., floor joists, wall studs, ceiling joists and rafters, and roof trusses, is 2 feet (610 mm). For instance, depending on the design floor loads and the allowable bending stress for a wood species and grade, 2x10 floor joists spaced at 24 inches (610 mm) on center may carry the same span that 2x8 floor joists spaced at 16 inches (406 mm) on center could carry. Two 2x10s cost less than three 2x8s, and there are one-third fewer framing members to be handled and installed than with the traditional 16-inch (406 mm) spacing. The number of fastenings required to attach sheathing or flooring materials to the framing is reduced by the same proportion. A 2-foot (610 mm) module has similar advantages in exterior wall construction. Where 2x4 studs spaced 24 inches (610 mm) on center are not adequate such as in two-story structures, 2x6 studs spaced 24 inches (610 mm) on center may be used with the added benefit that they allow thicker wall insulation.

The even 2-foot (610 mm) multiples also simplify the framing layout. Other modules may be used as well, such as the traditional 16-inch (406 mm) stud spacing with a 4-foot (1.22 m) module, as long as each structural member is appropriately engineered and existing material sizes are fully used. The 2-foot (610 mm) module, however, is generally the most cost-effective and provides greater flexibility in design. Carpenters and others will usually find it easier to think in terms of 2, 4, 6, and 8 feet instead of 16, 32, 48, 64, 80, and 96 inches, making field calculations simpler and reducing the chance for error.

Regardless of the module used, when all floor, wall, and roof framing is coordinated at the same spacing, the respective members bear directly over each other (see Figure 2.1). Dead and live loads are therefore transferred directly through the lower members to the foundation. The result is a more efficient structure and a reduction in or elimination of some framing members used to distribute loads (this is discussed further in Chapter 5).

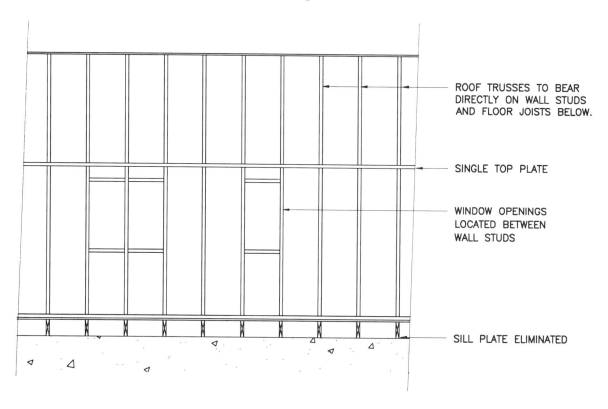

ROOF TRUSSES TO BEAR DIRECTLY ON WALL STUDS AND FLOOR JOISTS BELOW.

SINGLE TOP PLATE

WINDOW OPENINGS LOCATED BETWEEN WALL STUDS

SILL PLATE ELIMINATED

FIGURE 2.1 In-Line Framing Using Modular Spacing of Members

HOUSE CONFIGURATION

In cost-effective home design, preliminary layouts are prepared for the floor, wall, and roof framing early in the planning stage. This helps to determine the most economical plan configuration and provides a basis for developing the floor plan and exterior design.

Structural wood panels such as plywood and oriented strandboard are most commonly supplied in 4 x 8 foot (1.22 x 2.44 m) sheets. Because these building materials are produced in multiples of 4 feet (1.22 m), it follows that a plan that is laid out in multiples of 2 feet (610 mm) will permit the best use of floor, wall, and roof covering materials. The traditional 16-inch (406 mm) spacing requires a 4-foot (1.22 m) module. However, a 4-foot (1.22 m) module does not provide the flexibility that a 2-foot (610 mm) module does in residential design. Where cutting is necessary, the 2-foot (610 mm) module ensures that the resulting cutoff will be in some multiple of 2 feet (610 mm) for use elsewhere. A house laid out to use available materials to the fullest extent possible reduces waste and costs less per square foot.

A cost-effective plan should provide the best possible economy of enclosed area. A rectangular plan has only four corners joined by four straight walls and provides for simple floor and roof structures. The most effective rectangular shape is a square. It encloses the greatest amount of floor area for a given length of exterior wall. However, economical spans for the floor and roof systems tend to limit the depth of rectangular plans to a range between 24 and 32 feet (7.32 and 9.75 m). For cost-effective home building, the floor joists and roof rafters or trusses should run in the same direction and not exceed practical span limitations (see Chapters 4 and 6).

With a practical limit on plan depth, length may be extended to the dimension necessary to provide the desired rectangular floor area. For example, Table 2.1 lists a series of alternative rectangular shapes, each enclosing approximately 1,100 square feet (102 m²). Plan "C" represents a particularly efficient solution. It measures 28 x 40 feet (8.5 x 12.2 m) and is a multiple of 4 feet (1.22 m) in both directions. It encloses 1,120 square feet (104 m²) of floor area with a comparatively high ratio of floor area to linear feet of exterior wall. It provides for economical floor and roof spans, the length-to-depth relationship furnishes a desirable scale from a design standpoint, and the 28-foot (8.53 m) depth is a good dimension for interior layout.

TABLE 2.1
Ratio of Floor Area to Wall Length for Rectangular-Shaped Floor Plans
with area approximately 1,100 SF (102 m²)

PLAN	SIZE		FLOOR AREA		EXTERIOR WALL		RATIO FLOOR/WALL	
	Feet x Feet	Meters x Meters	Square Feet	Square Meters	Feet	Meters	Square Feet/Feet	Square Meters/ Meter
A	24x46	7.3x14.0	1104	102	140	42.67	7.89	2.39
B	26x42	7.9x12.8	1092	101	136	41.45	8.03	2.44
C	28x40	8.5x12.2	1120	104	136	41.45	8.24	2.51
D	30x36	9.1x11.1	1080	100	132	40.23	8.18	2.48
E	32x34	9.8x10.3	1088	101	132	40.23	8.24	2.51

Ref: *Reducing Home Building Costs with OVE Design and Construction.* NAHB Research Center, Upper Marlboro, MD. 1977.

A simple rectangular plan can accommodate a wide range of house styles and sizes. In combination with the 2-foot (610 mm) modular plan, it simplifies construction and ensures efficient material use. A deviation from the basic rectangle creates additional corners and reduces the ratio of floor area to linear feet of exterior wall. It also complicates floor and roof construction and requires additional labor and materials. The basic rectangle should be considered first and discarded reluctantly in cost-effective design.

Deviation from the basic rectangle can be achieved by cantilevering a portion of the floor over the foundation or a lower story. Cantilevering provides a relatively uncomplicated and inexpensive way to provide design variation. A cantilevered section does not alter foundation dimensions or spanning conditions of the floor system. In most cases, a 2-foot (610 mm) overhang is the most practical method to achieve design variation.

Another variation is to join two rectangles to form an L-shaped plan. Where used, an attached garage may be joined to a rectangular house to provide the effect of an L-shape without altering the house itself. The same dimensional principles apply to garages and carports. Plan configurations such as T-, U- or H-shapes involve numerous corners and complicated floor and roof constructions. They also add disproportionately to the cost. Floor and roof framing complications should be carefully considered and avoided, if possible.

LAYOUT OF INTERIOR SPACE

Cost-effective home building does not preclude practical and creative layout of interior space to define the rooms, closets, passageways, etc. The designer should exercise skill in preparing a series of preliminary layouts until the most functional scheme is found from the viewpoint of the anticipated home buyer. Development of an efficient floor plan takes careful planning.

Clear-span roof trusses provide an advantage. They permit interior nonload-bearing partitions to be located without regard to structural requirements. Roof trusses direct loads to exterior walls and eliminate the need for interior load-bearing walls.

Note that 2x3 studs may be used to frame nonload-bearing partitions. The cumulative additional usable floor area gained over conventional 4-inch (102 mm) partitions is significant. Other practical considerations should also be taken into account in locating and arranging partitions (see Chapter 7).

Room Size and Arrangement

A cost-effective room layout should be simple and uncomplicated, avoiding an excess of openings, corners, and offsets. The use of "open planning" in living areas helps reduce the total linear feet of partitions and creates a more spacious feeling, which is especially important in smaller homes.

Room sizes and other spatial dimensions vary widely depending on the size of the home and market preferences. For affordable housing, one important way to reduce the cost of a home is to reduce the size. Care should be taken, however, to satisfy the requirements of the local building code with regard to minimum dimensions for rooms, passageways, door openings, etc.

Stairway and Access Planning

Stairways and other openings that penetrate the floor or roof structure are particularly important in laying out the floor plan. Such openings should be located to interrupt the fewest possible number of structural members.

Straight-run stairs are the most cost-effective. They should be oriented parallel to floor joists so that, with 24-inch (610 mm) on center joist spacing, only one joist need be interrupted. Floor framing is further simplified if the stair opening is coordinated with the location of an existing joist on one side or the other. The stairway should never interrupt a structural beam or load-bearing wall.

The use of a 7-foot 6-inch (2.29 m) ceiling height (discussed in greater detail in Chapter 5) often permits a stair design with only 12 risers and 11 treads, which is one less riser tread than in a conventional 8-foot (2.44 m) ceiling height. The resulting shorter stair run affords greater flexibility when locating the stairs in tight design conditions.

Access openings to attics and crawl spaces should also be located to avoid interrupting framing members. The 2-foot (610 mm) on center spacing of framing members generally provides ample clearance for access between members. However, special planning is required to locate the opening in a closet, hallway, or other concealed location so that it may be located between framing members.

MECHANICAL AND ELECTRICAL REQUIREMENTS

A cost-effective plan should include provisions for the necessary plumbing, heating, and cooling systems. The vertical alignment of framing members simplifies the planning of mechanical risers such as ducts, vents, and plumbing stacks that must pass through the structure. Mechanical components should be planned to avoid interrupting structural members. Electrical requirements should also be considered during the planning stage to minimize wiring and accessory costs.

Plumbing facilities such as for the kitchen, laundry, bathrooms, and water heater should be clustered together as closely as possible on the plan to minimize piping runs. With proper planning, the kitchen, laundry, and bathrooms can all be served with a single vent stack. If a house has more than one story, bathrooms and plumbing facilities should be stacked vertically; special care should be taken to align walls in the different levels to provide a clear vertical path for the plumbing stack to the roof without interrupting structural members. Sometimes it is necessary to provide a 4- or 6-inch (102 or 152 mm) plumbing wall to accommodate the vent stack and other piping. It is best to avoid locating the plumbing in an exterior wall because of structural and insulation considerations. If it is possible to concentrate all or most plumbing in one single wall, a prefabricated plumbing "tree" may be considered.

Heating/cooling equipment should be placed in a central location on the floor plan to provide for good air distribution and to minimize duct runs (assuming a forced-air system). Equipment sizing and design of the system itself depend on heat loss and heat gain properties of the total house design. Specifications for insulation, windows, doors, etc., that reduce heating/cooling energy requirements are strongly recommended. This will result in smaller heating and cooling equipment and lower operating costs that contribute to the overall cost effectiveness of the house in the long term. Vertical or horizontal chases may be necessary for ducts, flues, or returns, which should be incorporated into the plan to avoid unforeseen complications. Vertical chases are especially important. Ample space for the necessary flues and ductwork is essential.

The electrical layout can be made more cost-effective by minimizing the number of switches, fixtures, and outlets and locating the switches close to fixtures. Threeway switches add to wiring costs and should be minimized. The service panel should be located close to the kitchen and/or utility area to minimize the length of heavy wiring runs.

EXTERIOR DESIGN

Generally, a functional no-frills treatment is encouraged for cost effectiveness. Where desired, however, any reasonable design (whether traditional or contemporary) can be used as long as the additional cost is consciously weighed and considered acceptable. Architectural design of the front exterior elevation is the major factor in determining the character of the house. While exterior design is an important cost factor, it is also a significant marketing factor.

A wide range of exterior architectural styles from contemporary to traditional can be used. A functional treatment is generally the most cost-effective because it avoids extraneous details and permits materials to be used to their best advantage. Additional costs of more detailed treatments should be carefully considered in relation to their market appeal. Traditional styles, where considered necessary, may often be achieved at relatively little extra cost.

Architectural Elements

Exterior design options relate primarily to the exterior walls and roof. The use of a clear-span trussed roof has significant benefits in cost-effective design. A straight gable trussed roof is the most cost-effective. However, truss systems accommodate other roof forms, such as a hip roof, where considered necessary for design variation. Roof framing and construction are discussed further in Chapter 6.

Architectural elements of concern in exterior walls include siding, windows, doors, and trim. Any nonstructural siding material may be used over a suitable sheathing; however, the most cost-effective exterior covering is a single-layer structural panel siding fastened directly to the studs (discussed in Chapter 5). Standard prehung doors and prefinished window units save installation time and are available in a wide variety of styles (see Chapter 7).

Horizontal sliders, double-hung or other window types produced in modular width increments also reduce cost by minimizing framing requirements. One method, which uses window units designed to fit between studs, is discussed in Chapter 5. Regardless of window size, wall framing is more cost-effective if door and window openings are coordinated with stud locations on at least one side. The number of door and window openings in the exterior wall should be minimized to reduce cost as well as energy loss. An effort should also be made to limit variations to two or three different window sizes.

Design Variation

Although standardization is an important means of controlling costs in production building, every unit does not need to look identical. There are many opportunities for variation that do not add substantially to costs. For example, houses can be oriented at different angles to the street with varied setbacks. House designs could have different roof types and pitches; the siding material may vary in color and texture; and different styles of doors and windows may be used.

WORKING DRAWINGS

A detailed set of working drawings should be a standard element of cost-effective design. The primary purpose of working drawings is to convey all information that is pertinent to building the house. Working drawings also provide the basis for material takeoffs, cost estimating, and subcontractor bidding, all of which are particularly important considerations in cost-effective home building.

Without fully detailed drawings, subcontractors may bid a job at a higher cost to cover any uncertainties. On the other hand, drawings should not be cluttered with information that does not pertain to the construction process and compromises legibility. It is especially important to avoid extraneous notes, calculations, details, etc., that might confuse the field trades.

Whether the drawings are prepared by an architect, engineer, designer, or builder, they should be easy to read and sufficiently detailed. Standard sheet sizes used for drawings of single-family home designs include 11 x 17 inches (279 x 432 mm), 18 x 24 inches (457 x 610 mm), and 24 x 36 inches (610 x 914 mm). The smaller size is convenient to use in the field but is difficult to read. The larger sheets are difficult to handle under job site conditions and may contain too many details per sheet, possibly contributing to confusion. A standard sheet size of 18 x 24 inches (457 x 610 mm) is generally the ideal size for single-family house plans.

A typical set of working drawings should include the following sheets:

1. Site Plan
2. Exterior Elevations
3. Floor Plan
4. Foundation Plan
5. Sections and Details
6. Framing Plans
7. Mechanical Layouts

In some cases, more than one item can be combined on a single sheet. In other cases, certain items may require more than one sheet. Insofar as possible, each sheet should include all information required for a particular trade or phase of construction. Details, dimensions, and notes for any given trade or operation should not be scattered throughout a set of drawings.

SPECIFICATIONS

The designer may or may not be called upon to develop a set of specifications for the materials and products required for each house design. The basic specifications for major items such as framing lumber, concrete, doors and windows, and heating/cooling equipment can be noted on the appropriate drawing.

Generally, the builder determines detailed specifications for flooring, cabinets, fixtures, and appliances. The specifications for these items can have a major impact on the building cost, and may be offered as options.

In developing a detailed list of specifications, it is advisable to adopt or develop a standard form to ensure that all pertinent items are considered in each case. A sample form is provided in Appendix B to assist in developing a set of specifications.

CHAPTER 3
FOUNDATION CONSTRUCTION

TYPES OF FOUNDATIONS

The construction of a cost-effective home begins with the foundation. The foundation may take many different forms but its purpose is always the same: to provide a sound, durable base on which to build the structure. Generally, as with other structural components of a house, foundations have been built for worst-case conditions regardless of the given conditions at a particular site. In many cases, worst-case assumptions have led to overdesign, and inefficient use of materials. Cost-effective foundation design follows an engineered approach so that a foundation will adequately support the structure without wasteful overdesign.

Different types of foundations respond to different needs based on climate, soil conditions, and market preferences. Basements have traditionally been constructed in colder climates where the frost line is several feet into the ground. Crawl spaces are often built where the market does not require a basement or in areas with a high water table. Slab-on-grade foundations are constructed primarily in warmer climates where frost is not a problem. Because of the diversity in needs and design methods, the most cost-effective foundation type must be determined on a case-by-case basis. Regardless of traditional practice in your locality, the different foundation options and their respective costs should be carefully considered to determine the most cost-effective foundation for a particular application.

This chapter presents a general discussion of three basic foundation types: basement, crawl space, and slab-on-grade. It then explores foundation design, alternative materials, and other variations on the three foundation types.

Basements

Full basements are common in many areas of the nation, especially in colder regions where the frost depth requires a deeper foundation. In addition, in regions with extended periods of cold weather, a basement offers additional space for indoor activities at a relatively low cost per square foot.

Concrete block and plain (unreinforced) concrete are the most common basement constructions. Other variations may, however, be considered. One variation is a conventional concrete foundation that bears directly on the soil without a traditional footing (see Stemwall Foundations later in this chapter). Another variation calls for reinforced concrete walls that can reduce the amount of concrete, although the cost of the steel and additional labor may exceed the savings in concrete. In still another variation, permanent wood foundations are being installed in some areas of the United States and Canada. A cost-effective basement design depends on several factors in any given case. Some types of construction may offer benefits such as a reduction in construction time, less dependency on weather, and a greater adaptability to site conditions. All factors should be carefully weighed in selecting the best basement construction for any particular set of conditions.

Cost-effective basement design requires consideration of the design loads to which the foundation will be subjected and the best way to support these loads. (Foundation design is discussed in more detail later in this chapter). Because basement walls typically extend to about 7 feet (2.13 m) below finish grade, an important factor in structural design is the lateral pressure of soil against the wall. As the depth of the foundation wall increases, the lateral soil pressure against the wall becomes greater. Basement walls are normally supported against the soil pressure by the basement floor at the bottom and by the first-story floor at the top. However, in some semi-basement constructions such as a split foyer design (sometimes called "raised ranch"), the basement wall may not extend all the way up to the first floor, in which case it is not laterally supported at the top.

Crawl Space Foundations

The most widely used crawl space construction is similar to that of a basement except that the foundation wall does not extend as far below grade. The crawl space foundation offers flexibility on sites with sloping terrain (see Figure 3.1). The depth of a crawl space foundation is usually determined by local frost conditions. Where the entire area enclosed by a crawl space foundation is excavated, the walls are subject to the same engineering design procedures as basements.

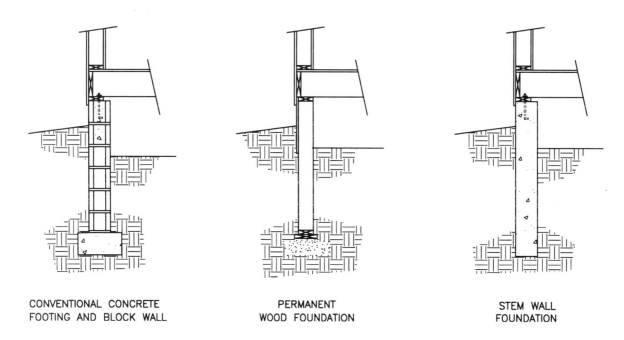

CONVENTIONAL CONCRETE
FOOTING AND BLOCK WALL

PERMANENT
WOOD FOUNDATION

STEM WALL
FOUNDATION

FIGURE 3.1 Crawl Space Foundations

Eighteen to twenty-four inches (457 to 610 mm) of headroom is generally adequate for access, unless greater headroom is desired to service mechanical equipment that may be located in the crawl space. Where the frost line requires a deeper footing, the walls may extend down below the level of the crawl space floor, thereby reducing the unbalanced height of backfill acting against the wall from the outside. This permits a less costly wall construction and is less prone to water problems.

As with basements, crawl space walls or footings are normally supported against lateral soil pressure by the first-story floor construction at the top; however, they lack the lateral support of a concrete slab floor at the bottom. Where walls extend below the floor level, the earth on the inside of the wall provides lateral support at the bottom. Where the entire crawl space area is excavated, it may be necessary to provide lateral wall support by some other means such as keying or anchoring to the footing. Lateral wall support can be important with deeper crawl space foundations where the soil pressure is greater.

Slab-on-Grade Foundations

Where the primary emphasis is on affordability, it may be advisable to consider a slab-on-grade foundation. Ground-supported concrete slabs are not subject to the span limitations of other floor constructions. Under suitable site conditions, concrete slab-on-grade construction often provides the most cost-effective foundation-floor combination.

There are, however, some practical limitations to concrete slab construction. The greatest limitation is topography. Concrete slab foundations are not well suited to sloping sites or other conditions that require a large amount of fill. The use of fill increases the chances of uneven settling and cracking. While concrete slabs may be supported on compacted fill or on intermediate piers, if the slab is properly reinforced, the added cost may favor a crawl space foundation.

Particularly in warmer climates, a monolithic concrete slab that combines the footings and floor in one pour is the least costly of all foundation types. The basic monolithic slab foundation consists essentially of a nominal 4-inch-thick (102 mm) concrete slab with a thickened edge (see Figure 3.2). The slab itself does not necessarily require reinforcing unless local experience dictates. However, one or two rebars are typically used at the thickened edge to assure against cracking and movement. In addition, where intermediate load-bearing walls require support, the slab thickness is normally increased and one or two rebars are installed. A concrete strength of 2,500 psi (17,237 kPa) is adequate under normal conditions. For areas with unstable soils, a special reinforced slab design should be determined with the assistance of a qualified engineer.

Cost-effective concrete slab foundations may be built in colder climates by insulating the foundation against ground frost with the use of frost-protected shallow foundations, which are discussed further on page 28. Heating ducts of one type or another are sometimes incorporated in slab-on-grade construction in colder climates. However, installation of these ducts can complicate construction and unnecessarily increase costs.

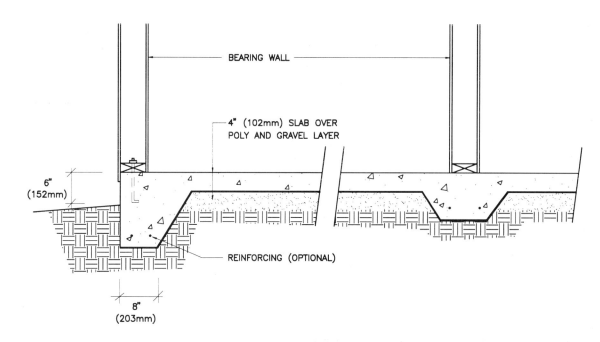

FIGURE 3.2 Monolithic Foundation Slab

FOUNDATION DESIGN

No matter what type of foundation is selected it is worth the effort to ensure that it is constructed to accurate dimensions and is level and square. Overall dimensions and layout should be in accordance with the modular planning guidelines as discussed in Chapter 2. It is usually better to hold the foundation dimensions slightly undersized, thereby permitting the balance of the structure to be built to the specified dimensions with a slight "overhang."

All foundations must be designed to distribute building loads to the underlying soil. Conventional footings are often over built. The most cost-effective footing size is one that balances the total building design load against the allowable bearing capacity of the soil. Basement and crawl space foundations need to resist the lateral earth pressure against the exterior side of the wall. Therefore, the following factors must be considered to ensure that a foundation wall or footing is engineered both properly and cost effectively:

- total live and dead design load of the building;
- allowable bearing capacity of the soil; and
- lateral earth pressure on the wall.

Design Loads

Before the footing or wall can be designed, the loads that may be transferred through the structural members to the foundation must be determined. The weight of the structure itself constitutes the dead load. Live loads include people, furniture, and other transient loads. Snow can add significantly to live loads in colder climates. Wind can also add significantly to live loads, especially in coastal areas, as well as introduce up-lift forces on the house structure. In other regions of the country, seismic loads need to be considered.

Dead, live, and snow loads are discussed briefly in this handbook. For areas where wind and seismic loads are of concern, additional guidance will be necessary from the local building department and from a qualified professional. Appendix C includes a Basic Wind Speed Map, Design Wind Load Table, and Seismic Risk Map.

Design loads for any building depend on the weight of the structure, as well as that of live loads based on the occupancy function of the building. The total design load, then, is determined by adding together the dead and live loads of the structure. These loads are usually assumed for engineering purposes and are included in the local or state building code. Figure 3.3 presents an example of residential dead and live loads. For wood-frame single-family homes, total design load at the base of the foundation wall or footing does not generally exceed 2,500 plf (36.5 kN/m) for one-story structures or 3,000 plf (43.8 kN/m) for two-story structures. Similarly, total design loads on center girder support columns do not generally exceed 7,000 lbs (31.1 N) for one-story structures, or 10,000 lbs (44.5 N) for two-story structures.

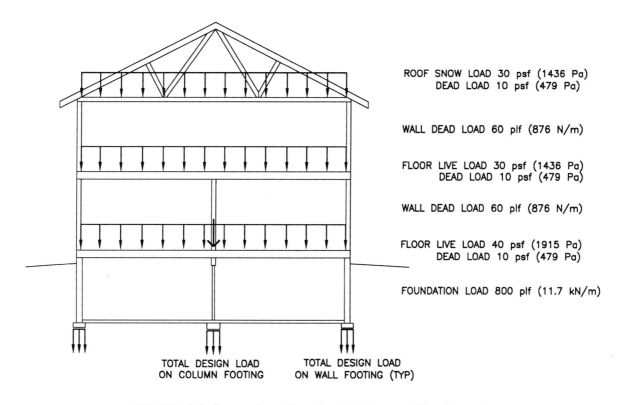

ROOF SNOW LOAD 30 psf (1436 Pa)
DEAD LOAD 10 psf (479 Pa)

WALL DEAD LOAD 60 plf (876 N/m)

FLOOR LIVE LOAD 30 psf (1436 Pa)
DEAD LOAD 10 psf (479 Pa)

WALL DEAD LOAD 60 plf (876 N/m)

FLOOR LIVE LOAD 40 psf (1915 Pa)
DEAD LOAD 10 psf (479 Pa)

FOUNDATION LOAD 800 plf (11.7 kN/m)

TOTAL DESIGN LOAD ON COLUMN FOOTING

TOTAL DESIGN LOAD ON WALL FOOTING (TYP)

FIGURE 3.3 Example of Residential Live and Dead Loads

The snow load varies considerably with region. Normally, the local building code dictates the design snow load. Figure C.3-a to C.3-c in Appendix C are maps of approximate snow loads for the United States.

Soil-Bearing Capacity

Soil-bearing characteristics can vary substantially from one location to another. Local soil characteristics are sometimes known with sufficient reliability to serve as a basis for footing design but are often substantially underrated. Where it is suspected that locally accepted values are substantially inaccurate, it may be advisable to obtain more detailed data from on-site tests conducted by a soils engineer. Typically, allowable soil-bearing capacities range between 1,500 and 5,000 psf (71.8 and 239 kPa). Soils with an allowable bearing capacity of less than 1,500 psf (71.8 kPa) are uncommon, while soils with bearing capacities of more than 5,000 psf (239 kPa) are not unusual. Special attention should be given to expansive soils. For areas where there is concern about soil conditions, the builder or designer is well advised to have an engineer perform a soils investigation.

Footing Design

Cost-effective residential footing design consists of balancing the design load per square foot of footing bearing area against the allowable load per square foot bearing capacity of the soil. In house design, a separate spread footing may not be necessary. A basement or crawl space wall itself may bear directly on the soil if the soil is adequate to support the design load of the structure (see page 23, Stemwalls). If a particular soil cannot support the wall by itself, a spread footing may be necessary. Table 3.1 provides footing widths for various building loads and soil capacities. Where separate footings are used, they should be at least 2 inches (51 mm) wider than the wall to provide field tolerance for wall placement.

TABLE 3.1
Minimum Bearing Width
for Continuous Load-Bearing Foundation Walls or Footings

BUILDING HEIGHT	SOIL BEARING CAPACITY															
	1500 psf	71.8 kPa	2000 psf	95.8 kPa	2500 psf	119.7 kPa	3000 psf	143.6 kPa	3500 psf	167.6 kPa	4000 psf	191.5 kPa	4500 psf	215.5 kPa	5000 psf	239.4 kPa
	in	mm	in	mm	in	mm	in	mm	in	mm	in	mm	in	mm	in	mm
CONVENTIONAL WOOD FRAME CONSTRUCTION																
1-Story	16	406	12	305	10	254	8	203	7	178	6	152	6	152	6	152
2-Story	19	483	15	381	12	305	10	254	8	203	7	178	7	178	6	152
3-Story	22	559	17	432	14	356	11	279	10	254	9	229	8	203	7	178
4" (102 mm) BRICK VENEER OVER WOOD FRAME OR 8" (203 mm) HOLLOW CONCRETE MASONRY																
1-Story	19	483	15	381	12	305	10	254	8	203	7	178	7	178	6	152
2-Story	25	635	19	483	15	381	13	330	11	279	10	254	9	229	8	203
3-Story	31	787	23	584	19	483	16	406	13	330	12	305	10	254	9	229

Where support is necessary under girders and center beams, column footings may be required. Table 3.2 shows column footing sizes for various design loads and soil-bearing capacities.

TABLE 3.2
Column Footing Sizes
dimension given is one side of a square footing

TOTAL DESIGN LOAD		ALLOWABLE SOIL-BEARING CAPACITY															
		1500 psf	71.8 kPa	2000 psf	95.8 kPa	2500 psf	119.7 kPa	3000 psf	143.6 kPa	3500 psf	167.6 kPa	4000 psf	191.5 kPa	4500 psf	215.5 kPa	5000 psf	239.4 kPa
lbs	N	in	mm	in	mm	in	mm	in	mm	in	mm	in	mm	in	mm	in	mm
4,000	17.8	20	508	17	432	15	381	14	356	13	330	12	305	12	305	11	279
6,000	26.7	24	610	21	533	19	483	17	432	16	406	15	381	14	356	13	330
8,000	35.6	28	711	24	610	22	559	20	508	18	457	17	432	16	406	15	381
10,000	44.5	31	787	27	686	24	610	22	559	21	533	19	483	18	457	17	432
12,000	53.4	34	864	30	762	27	686	24	610	22	559	21	533	20	508	19	483
14,000	62.3	—	—	32	813	29	737	26	660	24	610	23	584	21	533	20	508

The thickness of a standard concrete footing is controlled by the amount of projection beyond the wall, pier, or column that it supports. A footing thickness of at least 6 inches (152 mm) or the projection length on either side of the wall, whichever is greater, is common with 2,500 psi (17,237 kPa) concrete. The thickness may be reduced if the footing is properly reinforced. Reinforcing is often advantageous with larger column footings to reduce the thickness of the concrete.

The minimum depth of wall footings below grade is usually controlled by local frost conditions. Footings should extend to or below the frost line to prevent destructive heaving action of frozen soil (with the exception of frost-protected shallow foundations, see page 28). Other local factors such as groundwater and certain soil types may also affect footing requirements. Footings should normally extend down to original undisturbed soil. They may, however, bear on compacted fill as determined by a qualified engineer.

Foundation Wall Thickness

Where foundation walls extend 4 feet (1.22 m) or more below finish grade, the lateral pressure of soil against the wall becomes a major factor in structural design. As the depth of the foundation wall increases, the lateral soil pressure against the wall becomes greater. Figure 3.4 illustrates the relation of load to the height of the backfill. As discussed previously, basement walls are normally supported against the soil pressure by a concrete floor slab at the bottom and by the first-story floor at the top. However, in some constructions (outside of high wind areas and Seismic Zones 3 and 4), the foundation wall may not extend all the way up to the first floor, in which case it is not supported at the top. Also, in crawl spaces that are completely excavated, the bottom of the wall may not be supported.

Typical engineering practice assumes the soil pressure of a reasonably well-drained soil to be equivalent to a fluid weighing from 30 to 35 lbs./cubic foot (pcf) (481 to 561 kg/m³), although this may range to over 100 pcf (1,602 kg/m³) with groundwater or other adverse conditions. Basement walls in flood-prone areas may be subject to substantially greater loads and thus require special engineering solutions.

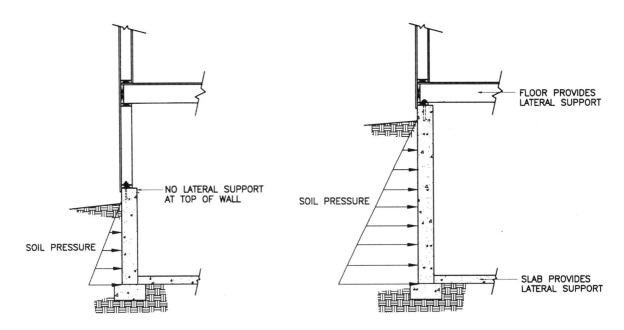

FIGURE 3.4 Earth Pressure Diagrams Showing Relation of Load to Height of Backfill

Foundation walls are specified in terms of the thickness required to support a particular height of backfill. Table 3.3 provides minimum thicknesses for plain concrete and concrete block foundation walls. Wall thicknesses may be reduced if they are designed with steel reinforcement by a qualified engineer.

TABLE 3.3
Thickness of Foundation Walls

FOUNDATION WALL CONSTRUCTION	THICKNESS[a]		MAXIMUM DEPTH OF UNBALANCED FILL[b]	
	Inches	Millimeters	Feet	Meters
Masonry of Hollow Units, Ungrouted	8	203	4	1.22
	10	254	5	1.52
	12	305	6	1.83
Masonry of Solid Units	6	152	3	0.91
	8	203	5	1.52
	10	254	6	1.83
	12	305	7	2.13
Masonry of Hollow or Solid Units, Fully Grouted	8	203	7	2.13
	10	254	8	2.44
	12	305	8	2.44
Plain concrete	6	152	6	1.83
	8	203	7	2.13
	10	254	8	2.44
	12	305	8	2.44
Masonry of Hollow Units, Reinforced Vertically with No. 4 Bars and Grout at 24 Inches (610 mm) on Center. (Bars located not less than 4½ inches [114 mm] from pressure side of wall.)	8	203	7	2.13

Note: This table is based on a minimum concrete strength of 2,500 psi (17,237 kPa) and standard hollow core load-bearing concrete block with type M or S mortar.
[a]The actual thickness may be up to ½ inch (13 mm) less than the required nominal thickness specified in the table.
[b]Maximum depths of unbalanced fill (height of finished ground level above basement floor or inside ground level) may be increased with the approval of the code official where soil conditions or local experience warrant such increase. Consult engineer for foundations in Seismic Zones 3 or 4.

Ref: *CABO One- and Two-Family Dwelling Code, 1992 Edition.* Council of American Building Officials, Falls Church, VA. 1992.

FORMED CONCRETE FOUNDATIONS

Plain concrete walls are usually formed on both sides and rest on a spread footing. They have a smooth or textured finish (e.g., brick) and provide good resistance to water infiltration. Special forms are available with an integral flared footing detail to increase bearing area at the bottom, although these special forms are limited to walls of 5 feet (1.52 m) in height or less as used in some split-foyer (raised ranch) house designs. Plain concrete constructions may have three or four reinforcing bars placed horizontally in the wall for control of shrinkage cracking.

In areas requiring design against seismic forces or where soil pressures generally exceed 30 pcf (481 kg/m^3), a reinforced wall may be required. Reinforced concrete construction has both horizontal and vertical reinforcing sized and positioned according to engineering requirements. Reinforcing requirements depend on wall thickness, backfill height, concrete strength, and other factors. Standard engineering design for reinforced concrete concentrates on heavy construction and the safety factors that are used can result in overdesign in light structures such as houses.

STEMWALL FOUNDATIONS

A stemwall foundation is a concrete foundation wall that transfers building design loads directly to the soil without a separate spread footing. The construction of a stemwall is similar to that of a conventional formed concrete wall built on a spread footing except that it is formed directly on the ground (see Figure 3.1). Stemwalls may also be trenched. A detailed design procedure and design tables are presented in the publication *Stemwall Foundations for Residential Construction* by the NAHB Research Center produced for HUD.[1]

CONCRETE BLOCK FOUNDATIONS

Basements constructed of concrete block have been used extensively because of the availability and relatively low cost of block, and versatility of concrete block wall construction. Concrete blocks are composed of Portland cement, fine aggregate, and water. Standard blocks are 8 inches (203 mm) high and 16 inches (406 mm) long—including the specified 3/8-inch-thick (10 mm) mortar head and bed joints. The size given for a block refers to its thickness. Standard block sizes are 8, 10, and 12 inches (203, 254, and 305 mm).

As with plain concrete walls, concrete block walls are specified in terms of minimum wall thickness to support a particular height of backfill (see Table 3.3). Hollow concrete blocks, which contain a double core in each block, are typically used in residential construction, although solid masonry block is occasionally used. The mortar mix for the block should be Type N for average strength or Type M for severe moisture conditions or stress. It is important to build a

---

[1]*Stemwall Foundations for Residential Construction.* NAHB Research Center. Prepared for the U.S. Department of Housing and Urban Development, Washington, DC. 1993.

concrete block wall on a level concrete footing. The top course of block is usually filled solid to support the weight of the structure and to embed the anchor bolts or straps that secure the floor structure.

The traditional method of waterproofing a concrete block foundation is to parge (stucco) it with two coats of Type S mortar and then apply a bituminous "waterproofing." This double protection usually stands up well except in cases of serious cracking accompanied by a groundwater problem. One concern with concrete block walls is their ability to support excessive soil pressures, especially in saturated soil conditions.

It is important to wait until the first floor is framed and anchored before backfilling a concrete block wall. Reinforced concrete block walls and concrete block pilasters may be used to increase the resistance to soil pressure. However, the addition of reinforcing steel is usually not cost-effective compared to the construction of a thicker wall. The *One- and Two-Family Dwelling Code*[1] gives reinforcing provisions for concrete block walls.

PERMANENT WOOD FOUNDATIONS

Permanent wood foundations have gained acceptance in many areas of the United States and Canada. Thousands of homes have been built with this method, which is accepted by the U.S. Department of Housing and Urban Development for its mortgage insurance programs. The American Forest & Paper Association has published design and construction information for this type of foundation.[2]

The preservative treatment for wood foundations must be in accordance with American Wood Preservers Association Standard AWPA C-22. Each piece of lumber or plywood must bear the AWPA stamp or that of another approved inspection agency. Lumber and plywood treated in this manner are highly durable. Not all pressure-treated lumber is suitable for use in permanent wood foundations and should have AWPA approval for use in these applications.

Permanent wood foundations offer several advantages. They can be constructed in the form of basements or crawl space walls. When used as basement walls (see Figure 3.5), they can enhance below-grade living conditions. Unlike concrete walls, wood foundations easily accommodate the installation of electrical wiring, insulation, and standard interior wall finish materials. The foundations can be prefabricated and are especially well suited to construction in cold or wet weather. Prefabricated panels can be erected rapidly on site, reducing construction time and eliminating weather-related delays. Given that carpenters erect the panels, fewer trades need to be coordinated. Where basement walls extend above grade, they are usually covered with the same siding materials as the house walls.

---

[1]*CABO One- and Two-Family Dwelling Code, 1992 Edition.*

[2]*Permanent Wood Foundation System: Design, Fabrication, and Installation Manual.* American Forest & Paper Association, Washington, DC. 1987.

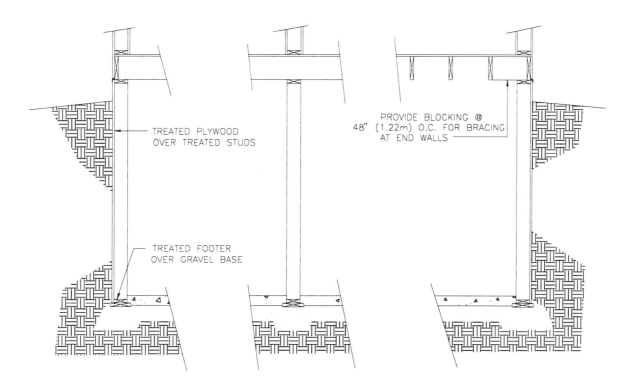

FIGURE 3.5 Permanent Wood Foundation System

Tables 3.4-a and 3.4-b summarize the typical framing requirements for different heights of fill and the typical footing plate sizes for one- and two-story houses up to 32 feet (9.75 m) in width. Studs are spaced 12 or 16 inches (305 or 406 mm) on center. A minimum of 1/2-inch-thick (13 mm) standard C-D grade (exterior glue) pressure-treated plywood should be installed with the face grain across the studs. Blocking at horizontal plywood joints is not required if joints are at least 4 feet (1.22 m) above the bottom plate. These specifications are based on soil conditions with 30 pcf (481 kg/m^3) equivalent fluid weight.

Fasteners used below grade in the treated wood should be stainless steel, silicon bronze, or copper types 304 or 316 as defined by the American Iron and Steel Institute classification. Hot-dipped zinc coated steel nails, if used, should have a minimum average zinc coating weight of 2 oz/ft^2 (9.76 kg/m^2) of surface conforming to ASTM A153.

Permanent Wood Basements

Construction of a permanent wood basement begins with excavation to the required level in the usual manner. Plumbing lines to be located below the basement floor are installed as necessary. The entire basement area is then covered with a minimum 4-inch-thick (102 mm) layer of crushed stone or gravel extending approximately 6 inches (152 mm) beyond the footing line. The stone or gravel bed is carefully leveled at all footing locations. Footing plates are then installed over the stone, which distributes footing loads to the soil. The wall panels are erected on the footing plates and fastened together and braced in place. Joints are caulked and the entire exterior surface below grade is draped with a continuous sheet of 6-mil (0.015 mm) polyethylene.

TABLE 3.4-a
Framing Requirements for Permanent Wood Foundations
for maximum 8-foot (2.44 m) basement walls with center-bearing floors

HEIGHT OF FILL		STUD AND PLATE SIZE	STUD SPACING		KEY TO LUMBER STRENGTH VALUES[1]								
Inches	Millimeters		Inches	Millimeters	Nonbearing Exterior Basement Wall Studs			Single-Story Roof Live Load of 30 psf (1436 Pa) and House Width of 32 Feet (9.75 m)			Two-Story Roof Live Load of 30 psf (1436 Pa) and House Width of 32 Feet (9.75 m)		
86	2,184	2x6	12	305	B-1	—	—	B-1	—	—	—	—	—
		2x8	16	406	B-2	C-1	D-1	B-2	C-1	—	B-2	C-1	—
			12	305	B-2	C-2	D-2	B-2	C-2	D-1	B-2	C-2	D-1
72	1,829	2x6	16	406	B-2	C-1	—	B-1	—	—	—	—	—
			12	305	B-2	C-2	D-1	B-2	C-1	—	B-2	C-1	—
		2x8	16	406	B-3	C-2	D-2	B-2	C-2	D-2	B-2	C-2	D-1
			12	305	B-3	C-3	D-2	B-3	C-2	D-2	B-3	C-2	D-2
60	1,524	2x4	12	305	B-1	—	—	—	—	—	—	—	—
		2x6	16	406	B-2	C-2	D-2	B-2	C-1	—	B-2	C-1	—
			12	305	B-3	C-2	D-2	B-2	C-2	D-2	B-2	C-2	D-1
		2x8	16	406	B-3	C-3	D-3	B-3	C-2	D-2	B-3	C-2	D-2
			12	305	—	—	—	B-3	C-3	D-3	B-3	C-3	D-3
48	1,219	2x4	16	406	B-2	C-1	—	—	—	—	—	—	—
			12	305	B-2	C-2	D-2	B-1	—	—	—	—	—
		2x6	16	406	B-3	C-3	D-3	B-3	C-2	D-2	B-2	C-2	D-2
			12	305	—	—	—	B-3	C-3	D-2	B-3	C-2	D-2
		2x8	16	406	—	—	—	B-3	C-3	D-3	B-3	C-3	D-3
36	914	2x4	16	406	B-3	C-2	D-2	B-2	—	—	—	—	—
			12	305	B-3	C-3	D-3	B-2	C-2	D-1	—	—	—
		2x6	16	406	—	—	—	B-3	C-3	D-3	B-3	C-3	D-2
			12	305	—	—	—	—	—	—	B-3	C-3	D-3
24	610	2x4	16	406	B-3	C-3	D-3	B-3	C-2	D-1	—	—	—
			12	305	—	—	—	B-3	C-3	D-2	—	—	—
		2x6	16	406	—	—	—	B-3	C-3	D-3	B-3	C-3	D-3

Notes: [1]See Table 3.4-b for key to required strength values.

Ref: *Permanent Wood Foundation System: Design, Fabrication, Installation Manual.* American Forest & Paper Association, Washington, DC. 1987. Used by permission of AFPA.

TABLE 3.4-b
Key to Strength Values for Permanent Wood Foundations

LUMBER KEY	MINIMUM ALLOWABLE DESIGN VALUES													
	F_b (Repetitive)				F_v		$F_{c\perp}$		F_c				E	
	2x6 2x8		2x4						2x6 2x8		2x4			
	psi	MPa	psi	MPa	psi	MPa	psi	MPa	psi	MPa	psi	MPa	psi	MPa
B-1	1,700	11.7	1,950	13.4	90	0.62	565	3.90	1,250	8.62	1,250	8.62	1,700,000	11,721
B-2	1,400	9.65	1,650	11.4	90	0.62	565	3.90	1,000	6.89	975	6.72	1,600,000	11,032
B-3	800	5.52	900	6.21	90	0.62	565	3.90	625	4.31	575	3.96	1,400,000	9.653
C-1	1,400	9.65	1,600	11.0	70	0.48	405	2.79	975	6.72	975	6.72	1,400,000	9,653
C-2	1,100	7.58	1,300	8.96	70	0.48	405	2.79	825	5.69	775	5.34	1,300,000	8,963
C-3	650	4.48	725	5.00	70	0.48	405	2.79	525	3.62	475	3.28	1,100,000	7,584
D-1	1,200	8.27	1,400	9.65	70	0.48	375	2.59	850	5.86	850	5.86	1,200,000	8,274
D-2	975	6.72	1,150	7.93	70	0.48	375	2.59	700	4.83	675	4.65	1,100,000	7,584
D-3	575	3.96	625	4.31	70	0.48	375	2.59	450	3.10	400	2.76	1,000,000	6,895

Notes: Allowable design values for lumber species and grades may be found in Appendices E and F, or in the *National Design Specification for Wood Construction*.

Ref: *Permanent Wood Foundation System: Design, Fabrication, Installation Manual.* American Forest & Paper Association, Washington, DC. 1987. Used by permission of AFPA.

A sump may be installed to ensure a dry basement. The stone or gravel bed is covered with 6-mil (0.015 mm) polyethylene, over which a standard 4-inch (102 mm) concrete floor slab is poured. The wood foundation should not be backfilled until the basement floor and the first-story floor are in place. The first-story floor must be securely fastened to the top of the wood basement walls to resist the inward force of backfill. Where soil pressure is substantial, it is advisable to use framing angles for the first-story connection. Solid blocking should be installed 48 inches (1.22 m) on center in the joist space at end walls to transmit foundation wall loads to the floor.

The granular layer around and under the footings and floor slab will drain any groundwater to the sump, therefore, a perimeter drain tile is not required outside the foundation wall. The space between the excavation wall and plywood sheathing should be backfilled with the same porous material used for the footings, to a height of 1 foot (305 mm) above the footing for well-drained sites or to one-half the total backfill height for poorly drained sites. Subsurface fabric drains may be substituted for the footing material. The rest of the excavation should be backfilled with the same type of soil that was removed during excavation, tamped in 6- to 8-inch (152 to 203 mm) layers. Heavy equipment should not be driven next to the wall during backfilling.

Permanent Wood Crawl Space

Crawl space foundation walls may also be constructed of pressure-treated lumber and plywood. Panels for crawl spaces are assembled in the same manner as for permanent wood basements using treated studs, plates, and plywood facing. However, because a crawl space requires no more than 24 inches (610 mm) of headroom, the 1/2-inch-thick (13 mm) plywood facing needs to extend only 2 feet (610 mm) down from the top plate to the level of the crawl space floor, while the unfaced studs can continue down to the frost line (except in high wind and seismic areas where the sheathing and studs should extend a minimum of 4 feet (1.22 m) into the ground to transfer the loads). Treated 2x4 studs may be spaced at 24 inches (610 mm) on center for single-story construction. For two stories, a spacing of 12 inches (305 mm) on center should be used.

Construction begins with excavation of the site to the level of the crawl space floor. If local frost conditions require a greater depth, a trench of appropriate width is dug around the perimeter so that the wall may extend down to the required depth. The bottom of the trench is then covered with a minimum 4-inch (102 mm) layer of crushed stone or gravel that is carefully leveled. Footing plates are placed on the stone or gravel. Wall panels are installed and braced in place; plywood joints are caulked; the wall is covered with 6-mil (0.015 mm) polyethylene below grade on the exterior.

A pressure-treated wood center-bearing wall may also be used. It can be assembled from 2x4 studs spaced at 24 inches (610 mm) on center. A plywood facing is not required. The wall may be supported on a stone or gravel bed in a shallow trench. As an alternative, center supports may be provided by a beam supported on columns or piers. For additional details on this type of foundation, contact the American Forest & Paper Association.

FROST-PROTECTED SHALLOW FOUNDATIONS

Recently, the use of frost-protected shallow foundations (FPSF) has been found to be a practical alternative to full basements in cold regions. The FPSF can significantly reduce the cost of constructing a home. In the Nordic countries over one million homes have been constructed using FPSFs over the last 30 years. A frost-protected shallow foundation relies on strategically placed insulation to raise the frost depth around a building, thereby allowing foundation depths as little as 12 inches (305 mm) in the most severe U.S. climates. Figure 3.6 illustrates a typical FPSF.

When properly designed and constructed, frost-protected shallow foundations can provide protection against frost heave equivalent to conventional foundations. The insulation reduces and redirects heat loss from the soil below and from the building to keep the underlying soil and foundation from freezing. FPSFs also work with unheated parts of buildings such as garages by trapping geothermal heat below the building.

Extruded or molded expanded polystyrene (EPS) insulation is placed around the foundation perimeter, using vertical insulation against the interior or exterior face of the foundation wall and horizontal insulation in the ground 2 to 4 feet (610 to 1219 mm) out from the wall. Horizontal insulation can be omitted in mild climates. The thickness of the required insulation depends on several variables. The key variables are the climate (including the freezing index and mean annual temperature), the frost susceptibility of the soil, the thermal conductivity of the soil, and the internal temperature of the building.

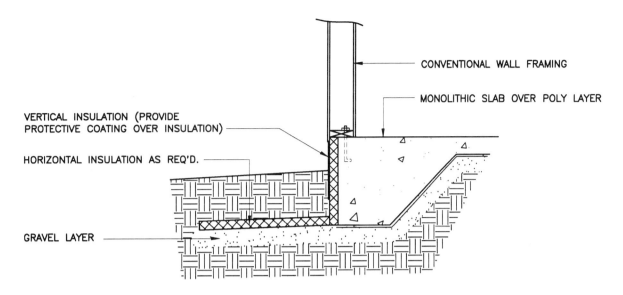

FIGURE 3.6 Frost-Protected Shallow Foundation

Ground insulation should be protected from excessive moisture to ensure its performance. A nonfrost-susceptible layer under the insulation in the form of a 4-inch-thick (102 mm) gravel bed is recommended to ensure the drainage around the insulation and foundation.

Continuity in insulation is also important. Gaps between sections of insulation should be avoided to prevent cold bridges that could result in localized frost heave or create cold spots in the slab floor.

A preliminary design procedure for FPSFs is included in the publication *Frost Protected Shallow Foundations in Residential Construction*, available from HUD.[1]

FOUNDATION DRAINAGE

The finished grade should always slope away from the foundation to divert surface water. Where groundwater or poorly drained soil is a potential problem, drain tile or gravel should be placed around the foundation at the base of the wall. The bottom of the drain tile or gravel should not be lower than the bottom of the footing or higher than the basement floor surface. Filter cloth may be used to cover the gravel to keep fine soil from infiltrating and blocking the pores. The collected water should be drained away from the foundation.

---

[1]*Frost Protected Shallow Foundations in Residential Construction.* NAHB Research Center. Prepared for the U.S. Department of Housing and Urban Development, Washington, DC. 1993.

INSECT INFESTATION AND DECAY

Where wood members are in proximity to the soil, termites and decay can be a problem for untreated wood. Appendix C includes a termite infestation probability map and a decay probability map of the United States. Where a probability of termite and decay damage exists, pressure-treated lumber should be used.

CHAPTER 4
FLOOR CONSTRUCTION

There are two basic types of floor construction commonly used in home building: concrete slab and wood frame. Concrete slab floors are addressed in Chapter 3.

Most wood-frame floors use nominal 2-inch-thick (51 mm) joists spaced at 16 or 24 inches (406 or 610 mm) on center, bearing on a center girder and covered with wood structural panels, including plywood and oriented strand board (OSB). While other variations of wood-frame floor construction are used in some regions, a wood joist system is generally the most universal and cost-effective floor construction.

This chapter focuses on cost-effective techniques for the construction of wood joist floor systems, including girders, joists, floor sheathing, and other related members. As discussed in Chapter 2, a 2-foot (610 mm) module is suggested for joist spacing. Other spacings may be used, but it is always best to coordinate with the spacing of wall and roof framing members.

SILL PLATE

A wood-frame floor system should be anchored to the foundation to resist wind and seismic forces acting on the structure. In conventional practice, a 2x6 sill plate is typically attached to the foundation with 1/2-inch (13 mm) anchor bolts and floor joists are toe-nailed to the sill plate.

However, sill plates may be eliminated where the top of a foundation is sufficiently level and accurate. Joists may bear directly on a solid concrete wall or on a top course of solid concrete block. They may also bear directly on hollow core concrete block on cores that have been filled with mortar (see Figure 4.1). Anchorage of the floor system may be provided by anchor straps or other devices that are embedded in the foundation wall in the same manner and at the same spacing as conventional anchor bolts. The straps should be spaced to coincide with joist locations so that each may be nailed directly to the side of a joist. They are fastened in the plane of the wall and are rated to resist the lateral forces the house may be subjected to with wind and seismic loads. A treated wood foundation does not require a separate sill plate or special anchor devices. Floor joists bear directly on the top foundation wall plate and are toe-nailed to provide anchorage.

Where a sill plate is preferred, a 2x4 member is generally adequate with either a solid concrete or a hollow core masonry foundation wall. The sill plate may be attached with anchor bolts or straps as described above. The straps do not require holes in the sill plate; metal tabs are simply bent up around the plate and nailed. Anchor straps are less exacting and do not interfere with other framing as conventional bolts often do.

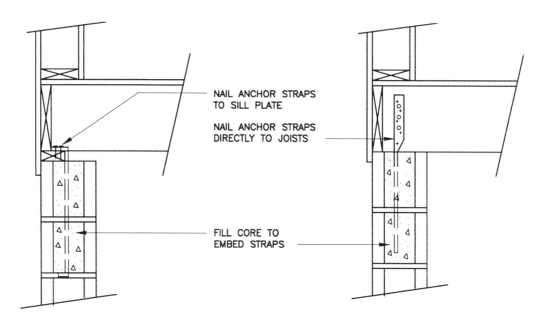

FIGURE 4.1 Sill Plate Reduced or Eliminated

GIRDERS

Wood-frame floor construction typically includes a center girder or support beam to provide intermediate support for the first floor. In two-story construction, the beam generally supports the second floor as well. The second-story load is transmitted to the first floor by means of a load-bearing wall extending down the center of the first story (see Figure 3.3).

For maximum benefit in reducing joist spans, girders and bearing walls should be located along the centerline of the structure. However, in some cases, it may be desirable to offset the girder 1 foot from the centerline to allow for even-length joists (e.g., use a 14-foot [4.27 m] and a 12-foot [3.66 m] joist as opposed to two 13-foot [3.96 m] joists in a 26-foot-deep [7.92 m] floor system) assuming that the offset does not result in the need for a larger joist size. It should be noted that this is not a limitation if off-center spliced joists are used as discussed later.

The girder usually bears on the foundation at each of its ends and is supported along its length by columns or piers. The spacing of columns or piers is adjusted to the spanning capability of the girder for a particular design load. Two basic types of girders are commonly used—wood or steel. Although steel is usually more costly, the decision on whether to use a wood or steel girder should be based on a comparison of the total installed cost, including intermediate support columns or piers, footings, etc. Other factors such as delivery, scheduling, and construction ease, are also considerations.

Built-Up Wood Girders

Wood girders are typically built by nailing together three or four layers of dimension lumber. End joints in members should be located within 12 inches (305 mm) of a support column or pier; end joints in adjacent members should be at least 16 inches (406 mm) apart.

Table 4.1 presents typical allowable spans for built-up wood girders. Dry lumber should be used to avoid shrinkage and warping. Given that floor joists may be nailed directly to the girder, a wood plate is not necessary over wood girders.

TABLE 4.1
Allowable Spans for Built-Up Wood Center Girders

WIDTH OF STRUCTURE Feet (Meters)	GIRDER SIZE	MAXIMUM CLEAR SPAN					
		ONE STORY		TWO STORY		THREE STORY	
		Feet-Inches	Meters	Feet-Inches	Meters	Feet-Inches	Meters
24 (7.32)	3- 2x8	6-7	2.02	4-11	1.50	4-1	1.25
	4- 2x8	7-8	2.33	5-8	1.74	4-9	1.44
	3- 2x10	8-5	2.57	6-3	1.92	5-3	1.60
	4- 2x10	9-9	2.97	7-3	2.22	6-1	1.84
	3- 2x12	10-3	3.13	7-8	2.33	6-4	1.94
	4- 2x12	11-10	3.61	8-10	2.69	7-4	2.24
26 (7.92)	3- 2x8	6-4	1.94	4-9	1.44	3-11	1.20
	4- 2x8	7-4	2.24	5-6	1.67	4-7	1.39
	3- 2x10	8-1	2.47	6-1	1.84	5-0	1.53
	4- 2x10	9-4	2.86	7-0	2.13	5-10	1.77
	3- 2x12	9-10	3.01	7-4	2.24	6-1	1.87
	4- 2x12	11-5	3.47	8-6	2.59	7-1	2.15
28 (8.53)	3- 2x8	6-2	1.88	4-7	1.39	3-10	1.16
	4- 2x8	7-1	2.16	5-3	1.61	4-5	1.34
	3- 2x10	7-10	2.38	5-10	1.78	4-10	1.48
	4- 2x10	9-0	2.75	6-9	2.05	5-7	1.71
	3- 2x12	9-6	2.90	7-1	2.16	5-11	1.80
	4- 2x12	11-0	3.35	8-2	2.49	6-10	2.08
32 (9.75)	3- 2x8	5-9	1.75	4-3	1.30	3-7	1.08
	4- 2x8	6-7	2.02	4-11	1.50	4-1	1.25
	3- 2x10	7-4	2.23	5-5	1.66	4-6	1.38
	4- 2x10	8-5	2.57	6-3	1.92	5-3	1.60
	3- 2x12	8-11	2.71	6-8	2.02	5-6	1.68
	4- 2x12	10-3	3.13	7-8	2.33	6-4	1.94

Notes:
1. Values are for a clear-span trussed roof, a load-bearing center wall on the first floor in two-story construction, and a load-bearing center wall on the first and second floors in three-story construction.
2. Spans based on a species and grade of lumber having an allowable bending stress F_b=1000 psi (6895 kPa) for repetitive members. See Tables in Appendices E and F.

Steel Girders

Steel beams are often used for girders because of their greater spanning capabilities and the elimination of shrinkage problems. Table 4.2 presents the allowable spans for common sizes of steel girders. Steel girders usually cost more and require an additional supplier. The girders are also heavier and more difficult to handle in the field. However, their greater spanning capability reduces the required number of columns or piers, which tends to offset the higher cost of the beam.

TABLE 4.2
Allowable Spans for Typical Steel Center Girders

WIDTH OF STRUCTURE Feet (Meters)	BEAM SIZE	MAXIMUM CENTER TO CENTER SPAN					
		ONE STORY		TWO STORY		THREE STORY	
		Feet-Inches	Meters	Feet-Inches	Meters	Feet-Inches	Meters
24 (7.32)	W 6x9	11-4	3.44	8-10	2.68	7-4	2.23
	W 8x10	14-0	4.27	10-5	3.17	8-7	2.62
	W 10x12	16-10	5.12	12-4	3.75	10-2	3.11
	W 12x14	19-7	5.97	14-5	4.39	11-11	3.63
	W 14x22	26-0	7.92	20-0	6.07	16-6	5.03
28 (8.53)	W 6x9	10-10	3.29	8-2	2.50	6-10	2.07
	W 8x10	13-2	4.02	9-8	2.96	8-0	2.44
	W 10x12	15-7	4.75	11-5	3.47	9-6	2.90
	W 12x14	18-2	5.55	13-5	4.08	11-0	3.35
	W 14x22	24-8	7.53	18-7	5.67	15-4	4.66
32 (9.75)	W 6x9	10-4	3.14	7-8	2.35	6-4	1.92
	W 8x10	12-5	3.78	9-1	2.77	7-6	2.29
	W 10x12	14-7	4.45	10-8	3.26	8-11	2.71
	W 12x14	17-0	5.18	12-6	3.81	10-5	3.17
	W 14x22	23-7	7.19	17-5	5.30	13-6	4.11
36 (10.97)	W 6x9	9-10	2.99	7-2	2.19	6-0	1.83
	W 8x10	11-8	3.57	8-7	3.11	7-1	2.16
	W 10x12	13-10	4.21	10-1	3.08	8-5	2.56
	W 12x14	16-1	4.91	11-10	3.60	9-8	2.96
	W 14x22	22-4	6.80	16-6	5.03	12-0	3.66

Notes: Live load for first floor is 40 psf (1915 Pa); for the second and third floors, 30 psf (1436 Pa). The spans assume clear span trussed roof construction (no attic or roof loads are included). Dead load is 10 psf (479 Pa) per floor.

Ref: *Residential Steel Beam and Column Load/Span Tables—Wide Flange Beams.* American Iron and Steel Institute, Washington, DC. 1993. Used by permission of AISI.

Where steel girders are used in conventional practice, a 2x6 wood plate is normally attached to the top surface by bolting or other means. Floor joists are then toe-nailed to the plate to anchor the floor and to provide lateral bracing for the girder. However, a plate may not be required if the floor joists are fastened to the girder by other means. A less costly method is to drive 10d or 12d nails into the bottom edge of joists and to clinch them around the steel girder flange.

Engineered Wood Girders

Engineered wood products such as glue laminated, laminated veneer, and parallel strand lumber are becoming more popular in residential construction as the cost of solid lumber increases. These products make efficient use of material by using advances in adhesives and wood processing technology to provide products that have increased uniformity and dimensional stability.

The manufacturing of most engineered wood products removes or disperses weaknesses such as knots, and reassembles the material into higher-quality products. The resulting members have more uniform structural properties, a lower moisture content, and are less prone to shrinking and warping than solid lumber. They also allow greater lengths, widths, and thicknesses not possible with solid lumber. Table 4.3 provides a comparison of the relative strengths of some of these products. The manufacturer should be consulted for design properties of a particular engineered wood product.

TABLE 4.3
Relative Strengths of Engineered Wood Products

ENGINEERED WOOD PRODUCT	FIBER STRESS IN BENDING F_b		TENSION PARALLEL TO GRAIN F_t		SHEAR PARALLEL TO GRAIN F_v		COMPRESSION PERPENDICU- LAR TO GRAIN $F_{c\perp}$		COMPRESSION PARALLEL TO GRAIN F_c		MODULUS OF ELASTICITY E	
	psi	kPa	psi	kPa	psi	kPa	psi	kPa	psi	kPa	psi	kPa
Parallel Strand Lumber[1]	2950	20340	2400	16547	290	1999	600	4137	2900	19995	2,000,000	13,789,520
Laminated Veneer Lumber[2]	2875	19822	1850	12755	285	1965	500	3447	2700	18616	2,000,000	13,789,520
Glue Laminated Lumber[3]	1600-2400	11032-16547	650-1300	4482-8963	90-200	621-1379	300-600	2068-4137	900-1750	6205-12066	1,100,000-1,800,000	7,584,236-12,410,568

Notes: [1]Parallam PSL, 2x10
[2]MicroLam, 2x10
[3]Consult National Design Specification by American Forest & Paper Association (AFPA) for design values and adjustment factors for specific grades of Glue Laminated Lumber.

Ref: *Alternatives to Lumber and Plywood in Home Construction.* NAHB Research Center. Prepared for the U.S. Department of Housing and Urban Development, Washington, DC. 1993.

Glue-laminated members (glulams) consist of 1- or 2-inch-thick (25 or 51 mm) lumber that is glued together in layers to provide the required structural shape and size. The grain of all laminations is parallel to the length of the members. Glulams are manufactured to design values found in the national standard ANSI/AITC A190.1-1985.

Laminated veneer lumber is manufactured from veneers about 1/8-inch-thick (3 mm) that are laminated together with the grain of all laminates parallel to the length of the member. This product is manufactured in a continuous billet up to 1-3/4 inches (44 mm) thick and 4 feet (1.22 m) wide. The billet is then cut to the widths needed for joists, beams, or headers.

Parallel strand lumber is manufactured from thin veneers that are clipped into 1/2-inch-wide (13 mm) strands. The strands are combined with adhesives to form large billets that are typically 12 inches (305 mm) wide and range in thickness from 1-3/4 to 7 inches (44 to 178 mm). The billets are then sawn to the desired sizes.

COLUMNS

Columns used to support wood or steel girders are typically 3-inch (76 mm) steel pipe or lolly columns, although 4x4 or 6x6 timbers may also be used depending on the tributary area and design loads. Table 4.4 shows the maximum column spacing for typical wood and steel columns that have a maximum unsupported length of 8 feet (2.44 m).

TABLE 4.4
Maximum Spacing for Typical Wood and Steel Columns
for Support of Center Beams

WIDTH OF STRUCTURE Feet (Meters)	COLUMN SIZE	MAXIMUM SPACING					
		ONE STORY		TWO STORY		THREE STORY	
		Feet-	Meters	Feet-Inches	Meters	Feet-Inches	Meters
24 (7.32)	4x4 wood	8-4	2.53	4-7	1.40	—	—
	6x6 wood	20-2	6.16	11-2	3.41	7-10	2.38
	3" diameter STD	25-2	7.68	13-7	4.15	9-4	2.83
	TS 3x3x0.1875	27-4	8.32	14-10	4.51	10-1	3.08
	3.5" diameter STD	34-7	10.55	18-8	5.70	12-10	3.90
28 (8.53)	4x4 wood	7-1	2.16	4-0	1.22	—	—
	6x6 wood	17-4	5.27	9-7	2.93	6-7	2.01
	3" diameter STD	21-8	6.61	11-10	3.60	8-1	2.47
	TS 3x3x0.1875	23-6	7.16	12-10	3.90	8-10	2.68
	3.5" diameter STD	29-10	9.08	16-2	4.94	11-1	3.38
32 (9.75)	4x4 wood	6-4	1.92	—	—	—	—
	6x6 wood	15-1	4.60	8-5	2.56	5-10	1.77
	3" diameter STD	19-1	5.82	10-5	3.17	7-1	2.16
	TS 3x3x0.1875	20-8	6.31	11-4	3.44	7-8	2.35
	3.5" diameter STD	26-2	7.99	14-4	4.36	9-10	2.99
36 (10.97)	4x4 wood	5-7	1.71	—	—	—	—
	6x6 wood	13-5	4.08	7-6	2.29	5-2	1.58
	3" diameter STD	17-0	5.18	9-4	2.83	6-5	1.95
	TS 3x3x0.1875	18-5	5.61	10-1	3.08	6-11	2.10
	3.5" diameter STD	23-5	7.13	12-10	3.90	8-10	2.68

Notes: Live load for first floor is 40 psf (1915 Pa); for the second and third floors, 30 psf (1436 Pa).
Dead load is 10 psf (479 Pa) per floor. A clear span trussed roof is assumed; no attic or roof loads are included.
The unbraced length of column is 8 feet (2.44 m).
Wood columns are limited by column compression buckling. Values are not applicable to adjustable height columns.

Ref: For Pipe and Tube Columns: *Residential Steel Beam and Column Load/Span Tables—Pipe and Tube Columns*. American Iron and Steel Institute, Washington, DC. 1993. Used by permission of AISI.

FLOOR JOISTS

As discussed in Chapter 2, modular spacing of floor joists in coordination with other framing members is recommended to optimize material use. In addition, in-line positioning of joists over the girder is recommended to allow joists on both sides of the beam to be located precisely on module without the 1-1/2-inch (38 mm) offset that results with conventional lapped joists.

Where conventional joist lengths are installed in-line with joist ends butted over the girder, each joist must have at least a 1-1/2-inch (38 mm) bearing. It is usually necessary to cut each joist to the proper length to accommodate the bearing. In addition, the butted ends must be tied together with a wood or metal plate or in some other manner. If a structural splice is used to join the two joist ends, the end joint does not necessarily have to be located over the center support. If properly located, such an "off-center" splice can actually contribute to the allowable span (see Off-Center Spliced Joist Design, p. 38). It should be possible to obtain preassembled, precut in-line joists from a truss fabricator. On the other hand, it may be possible to obtain structural end-jointed lumber or other engineered wood members for full-length joists with no splices. Either of these variations of full length in-line joists may be installed more rapidly and accurately than conventional joists.

Regardless of the joist design used, floor deflection is decreased by gluing the plywood floor in place as discussed in Glued Floor Design. In most cases, floor joists may also be cantilevered over the foundation or a lower story by at least 2 feet (610 mm) to increase their effective span.

Conventional Joist Design

Existing span tables for floor joists provide allowable spans for 12-, 16-, 19.2-, or 24-inch (305, 406, 488, or 610 mm) on-center joist spacings. Allowable spans for a given size of joist at a given spacing depend on the strength properties of the wood and the design load.

A dead load of 10 psf (479 Pa) is generally assumed for wood-frame floors. The standard live load used for single-story homes or the first floor of two-story homes is 40 psf (1.92 kPa). A 30 psf (1.44 kPa) live load is often used for the second story of two-story homes, assuming lighter load conditions in bedroom areas. This should be checked with the local code.

The strength properties of wood depend on the species and grade of wood. The American Forest & Paper Association produces the National Design Specification (NDS®) for Wood Construction,[1] which includes design values for structural sawn lumber and structural glue laminated timber. Appendices E and F present strength properties of common species and grades from a supplement to the 1991 edition of the NDS®. Using these design values for the selected species and grade permits the determination of allowable clear spans. Table 4.5 shows allowable clear spans for conventional joists spaced at 16 and 24 inches (406 and 610 mm) on center.

Glued Floor Design

When a plywood or other wood structural panel subfloor is properly glued to floor joists with a construction adhesive, the panel and joists act together as a single structural member. The composite T-beam thus formed increases the stiffness of the plywood between joists.[2]

---

[1]*National Design Specification Supplement, Design Values for Wood Construction.* American Forest and Paper Association, Washington, DC. 1991.

[2]*Performance of Glued Single-Layer Plywood-to-Wood Joist Floor Systems.* NAHB Research Center. Prepared for the U.S. Department of Housing and Urban Development, Washington, DC. 1973.

TABLE 4.5
Allowable Spans for Floor Joists

JOIST			MODULUS OF ELASTICITY, E, IN 1,000,000 psi OR kPa											
SIZE	SPACING		1.0 psi	6.9 kPa	1.2 psi	8.3 kPa	1.4 psi	9.6 kPa	1.6 psi	11.0 kPa	1.8 psi	12.4 kPa	2.0 psi	13.8 kPa
	inches	mm	ft-in	m	ft-in	m	ft-in	m	ft-in	m	ft-in	m	ft-in	m
			30 psf (1436 Pa) LIVE LOAD											
2x6	16	406	9-2	2.79	9-9	2.97	10-3	3.12	10-9	3.28	11-2	3.40	11-7	3.53
	24	610	8-0	2.44	8-6	2.59	8-11	2.72	9-4	2.84	9-9	2.97	10-1	3.07
2x8	16	406	12-1	3.68	12-10	3.91	13-6	4.11	14-2	4.32	14-8	4.47	15-3	4.65
	24	610	10-7	3.23	11-3	3.43	11-10	3.61	12-4	3.76	12-10	3.91	13-4	4.06
2x10	16	406	15-5	4.70	16-5	5.00	17-3	5.26	18-0	5.49	18-9	5.72	19-5	5.92
	24	610	13-6	4.11	14-4	4.37	15-1	4.60	15-9	4.80	16-5	5.00	17-0	5.18
2x12	16	406	18-9	5.72	19-11	6.07	21-0	6.40	21-11	6.68	22-16	6.96	23-7	7.19
	24	610	16-5	5.00	17-5	5.31	18-4	5.59	19-2	5.84	19-11	6.07	20-8	6.30
$F_b$psi (kPa)	16	406	889	6129	1004	6922	1112	7667	1216	8384	1315	9067	1411	9729
	24	610	1018	7019	1149	7922	1273	8777	1392	9598	1506	10384	1615	11135
			40 psf (1915 Pa) LIVE LOAD											
2x6	16	406	8-4	2.54	8-10	2.69	9-4	2.84	9-9	2.97	10-2	3.10	10-6	3.20
	24	610	7-3	2.21	7-9	2.36	8-2	2.49	8-6	2.59	8-10	2.69	9-2	2.79
2x8	16	406	11-0	3.35	11-8	3.56	12-3	3.73	12-10	3.91	13-4	4.06	13-10	4.22
	24	610	9-7	2.92	10-2	3.10	10-9	3.28	11-3	3.43	11-8	3.56	12-1	3.68
2x10	16	406	14-0	4.27	14-11	4.55	15-8	4.78	16-5	5.00	17-0	5.18	17-8	5.38
	24	610	12-3	3.73	13-0	3.96	13-8	4.17	14-4	4.37	14-11	4.55	15.5	4.70
2x12	16	406	17-0	5.18	18-1	5.51	19-1	5.82	19-11	6.07	20-9	6.32	21-6	6.55
	24	610	14-11	4.55	15-10	4.83	16-8	5.08	17-5	5.31	18-1	5.51	18-9	5.72
$F_b$psi (kPa)	16	406	917	6322	1036	7143	1148	7915	1255	8653	1357	9356	1456	10039
	24	610	1050	7239	1186	8177	1314	9060	1436	9901	1554	10714	1667	11494

Note: The required bending design value F_b (psi or kPa) is shown at the bottom of the tables and is applicable to all lumber sizes shown. See Appendices E and F for design values for different species and grades of lumber.
Allowable spans are based on a deflection of L/360 at design load.

Ref: *Span Tables for Joists and Rafters*. American Forest & Paper Association, Washington, DC. 1993. Used by permission of AFPA.

Glue-nailing of the subfloor is recommended as a cost-effective method of increasing the stiffness of a floor. Glue-nailing is also highly effective in reducing floor squeaks, which may otherwise occur at a later time due to shrinkage of joists. Bounce and nail-popping may also be eliminated using this system. If OSB panels with sealed surfaces and edges are to be glued, check with the panel manufacturer for acceptable types of solvent-based glues that may be used.

Off-Center Spliced Joist Design

If two unequal joist lengths are spliced together so that the splice occurs at the point of minimal bending stress, spans for a given size of joist may be increased significantly. This arrangement provides structural continuity over the girder as compared to the use of individual joists, which end at the girder (see Figure 4.2). Under uniform load conditions on a continuous two-span joist of this type, the plate location is usually established at a point between one-fourth and one-third of the span from either side of the girder. This location must be determined on a case-by-case basis, however, because of the possibility of having unbalanced uniform loads over each of the spans. The splice location is therefore subjected to minimal bending stress and permits the use of a splice with less moment resistance than the joist itself. The splice may be formed with plywood or metal plates applied to both sides of the joist. For 2x8 joists, a 6 x 12-inch (152 x 305 mm) metal truss plate is adequate under normal load conditions.

Research conducted by the NAHB Research Center developed an off-center spliced joist design method, including design tables and a fabrication guide. Spliced joists for typical house widths may be fabricated from standard lengths of lumber as shown in Figure 4.2. Additional information and complete span tables are provided in *NAHB Research Report No. 4, Off-Center Spliced Floor Joists*[1]. Local building officials should be consulted to see if off-center spliced joists can be accepted in your area.

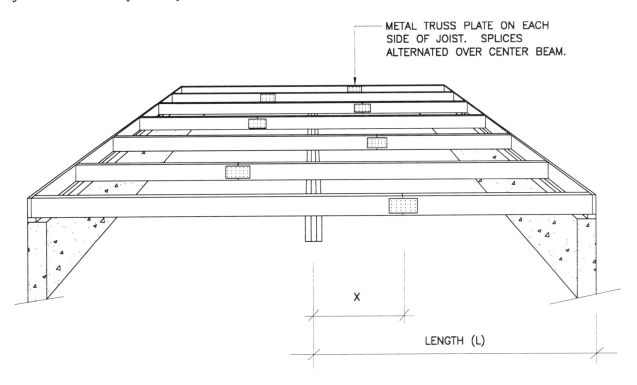

FIGURE 4.2 Off-Center Spliced Joists

Engineered Wood Joists

As with girders, engineered wood products have floor framing applications[2]. In particular, the long lengths, larger sizes, and greater spanning capabilities offer an advantage in certain

---

[1]*NAHB Research Report No. 4, Off-Center Spliced Floor Joists*. NAHB Research Center. Prepared for the National Association of Home Builders, Washington, DC. 1982.

[2]*Alternatives to Lumber and Plywood in Home Construction*. NAHB Research Center. Prepared for the U.S. Department of Housing and Urban Development, Washington, DC. 1993.

conditions. Laminated veneer lumber, wood I-beams, and wood floor trusses may be considered for use in floor framing. Since the structural properties of these products vary, manufacturers should be consulted for design values and span tables.

Laminated veneer lumber, as discussed on p. 35, comes in thicknesses up to 1-3/4 inches (44 mm) and may be used as a direct substitute for conventional floor joists.

Wood I-beams are typically made from solid lumber or laminated veneer flanges grooved to receive a plywood or OSB web. Wood I-beams are light in weight (about 2 plf [29.2 N/m]) and easy to handle. The flanges are available in a range of depths that offer a greater spanning capacity. Some I-beams have prescored knockout holes in the flanges for plumbing and electrical lines.

Floor trusses come in many varieties, from all-wood members fastened together with metal truss plates to composite trusses with steel webs. Floor trusses are available in a wide range of depths that can clear span typical house depths. Plumbing, duct work, and electrical wiring are easily installed through the open webs.

Joist Bridging

Cross bridging or solid blocking between joists is still used in some conventional construction. However, such bridging when improperly installed does not contribute to the performance of the floor and, in fact, may detract from floor performance by creating floor squeaks. Bridging is no longer required by the major model codes in normal residential floors and may be totally eliminated between floor joists up to and including 2x12s. However, where in-line joists are used and in high wind and seismic areas, bridging will help prevent the rolling over of joists.

Band Joists

The band joist used across the ends of floor joists has traditionally been the same size as its companion floor joists. One function of a band joist is to brace floor joists in position before application of the subfloor. The band joist also provides lateral support to joists, and helps support vertical loads in conventional construction where wall studs do not necessarily align with floor joists, or where I-joists (which are limited in compression) are used. This is important in high wind and seismic areas.

With modular planning, however, each wall stud bears directly over a floor joist. A nominal 1-inch-thick (25 mm) band may therefore be used in place of the traditional band joist to provide lateral support and positioning of joists. A 1x band uses less material and may be easily installed with 8d nails (see Figure 4.3).

In certain cases, the band joist may be entirely eliminated. Where a sill plate is used, it positions the bottom edge of the joists that are toe-nailed to it. The top edge of the joists may be aligned and fastened as the subfloor is installed, precluding the necessity for a band altogether. However, the siding and/or wall sheathing must extend down over the open joist ends as shown in Figure 4.3. Blocking or bridging of joists should be considered where band joists are eliminated.

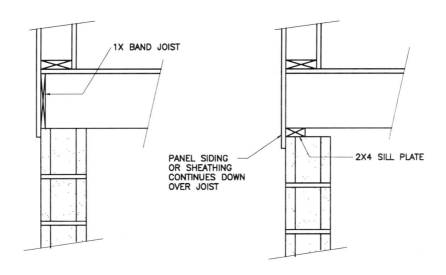

1X BAND JOIST

PANEL SIDING
OR SHEATHING
CONTINUES DOWN
OVER JOIST

2X4 SILL PLATE

FIGURE 4.3 Band Joist Reduced or Eliminated

FRAMING OPENINGS

Floor joists spaced at 2 feet (610 mm) on center provide ample clearance for mechanical ducts, crawl space access doors, and other smaller openings in the floor. If properly planned to occur between joists, the required opening may be framed with simple 2x4 blocking, leaving structural joists intact.

Larger openings such as stairwells may require disruption of one or more joists. Such openings should be planned so that their long dimension is parallel with the joists, thereby minimizing the number of joists that are interrupted. Special care should also be exercised at stair openings to avoid extending such openings through a center girder or bearing partition that supports a floor. Where possible, the opening should be coordinated with the normal joist spacing on at least one side to avoid the necessity for an additional trimmer joist to form the opening.

A single header is generally adequate for openings up to 4 feet (1.22 m) in width. A single trimmer joist at each side of the opening is usually adequate to support single headers that are located within a nominal 3 feet (0.91 m) of the end of the trimmer joist span (See Figure 4.4). Tail joists under 6 feet (1.83 m) in length may be fastened to a header with three 16d end nails and two 10d toe nails or equivalent nailing. Tail joists over 6 feet (1.83 m) in length should be attached with joist hangers. The header should be connected to trimmer joists by the same means that tail joists are connected to the header.

Where wider openings are unavoidable, double headers are generally adequate up to 10 feet (3.05 m) as shown in Figure 4.5. Tail joists may be connected to double headers in the same manner and under the same conditions as specified above for single headers. Tail joists that are end-nailed to a double header should be nailed before installation of the second member of the double header to provide adequate nail penetration into the tail joist. A double header should always be attached to trimmer joists with a joist hanger.

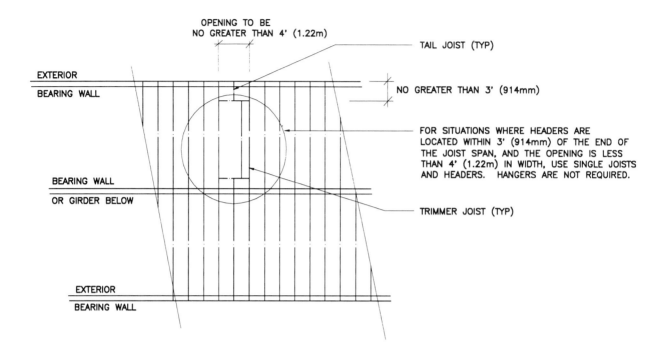

OPENING TO BE
NO GREATER THAN 4' (1.22m)

TAIL JOIST (TYP)

EXTERIOR

BEARING WALL

NO GREATER THAN 3' (914mm)

FOR SITUATIONS WHERE HEADERS ARE
LOCATED WITHIN 3' (914mm) OF THE END OF
THE JOIST SPAN, AND THE OPENING IS LESS
THAN 4' (1.22m) IN WIDTH, USE SINGLE JOISTS
AND HEADERS. HANGERS ARE NOT REQUIRED.

BEARING WALL

OR GIRDER BELOW

TRIMMER JOIST (TYP)

EXTERIOR

BEARING WALL

FIGURE 4.4 Single Header Used across Openings Less than 4 Feet (1.22 m) in Width

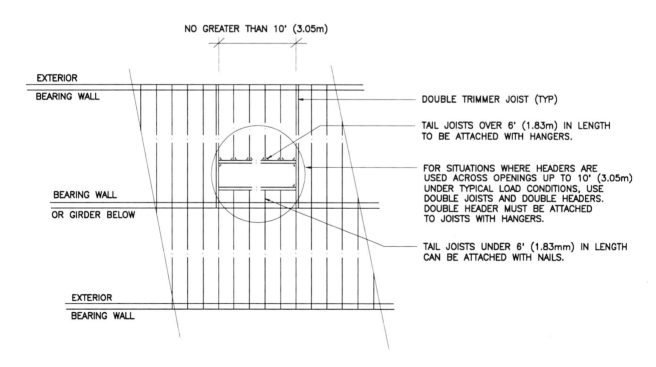

NO GREATER THAN 10' (3.05m)

EXTERIOR

BEARING WALL

DOUBLE TRIMMER JOIST (TYP)

TAIL JOISTS OVER 6' (1.83m) IN LENGTH
TO BE ATTACHED WITH HANGERS.

FOR SITUATIONS WHERE HEADERS ARE
USED ACROSS OPENINGS UP TO 10' (3.05m)
UNDER TYPICAL LOAD CONDITIONS, USE
DOUBLE JOISTS AND DOUBLE HEADERS.
DOUBLE HEADER MUST BE ATTACHED
TO JOISTS WITH HANGERS.

BEARING WALL

OR GIRDER BELOW

TAIL JOISTS UNDER 6' (1.83mm) IN LENGTH
CAN BE ATTACHED WITH NAILS.

EXTERIOR

BEARING WALL

**FIGURE 4.5 Double Header Used Across Openings up to 10 Feet (3.05 m) Under Typical Load
Conditions**

Trimmer joists at floor openings must be designed to support the concentrated loads imposed by headers where they attach to the trimmer. As noted previously, a single trimmer is adequate to support a single header located near the end of the span. All other trimmers should be at least doubled or should be engineered for specific design conditions.

SINGLE-LAYER FLOORING

In the past, conventional practice called for double-floor construction consisting of subfloor and finish floor or underlayment. However, where wall-to-wall carpet or resilient flooring is used, a single layer of underlayment grade plywood or wood structural panel with a tongue and groove edge may be applied directly to the floor joists. A substantial savings in labor and material is possible by combining functions in one material.

Wood structural panels such as plywood and OSB are most commonly used for floor sheathing. With the complexity and number of wood panels on the market today, the builder should make certain that the panel selected for use is approved for the application. A 3/4-inch-thick (19 mm) underlayment grade structural wood panel is usually adequate for single-layer floors installed over joists spaced 2 feet (610 mm) on center. However, the manufacturer's design tables should be checked to verify allowable spans and thicknesses of material to be used. Either 8d common nails or 6d deformed shank nails may be used. Nails should be spaced 6 inches (152 mm) apart at panel ends where they meet over a joist and 10 inches (254 mm) apart across the panel face.

Although nailing provides adequate attachment, the use of a construction adhesive offers additional benefits for application of single-layer structural wood panels. As discussed earlier under Glued Floor Design, glue-nailing of the panel floor to joists increases the stiffness of the floor system as well as the stiffness of the panel between joists. In addition, glue-nailing eliminates or reduces squeaks that can otherwise develop with even a small amount of joist shrinkage.

SUPPORTING NONLOAD-BEARING PARTITIONS

Double-floor joists are typically specified under nonload-bearing partitions that run parallel to the floor joists. However, 5/8-inch (16 mm) or 3/4-inch (19 mm) subflooring is adequate to carry such partitions between joists unless some extraordinary condition exists. In these cases, nonload-bearing parallel partitions may be nailed directly to the subfloor with no additional floor framing (see Figure 4.6).[1]

Partitions parallel to the overhead floor or roof framing may be anchored at the top by using 2x3 or 2x4 blocking installed flat and spaced 2 feet (610 mm) apart to provide backing for ceiling

---

[1]*Technical Note No. B 429, "Non-Load Bearing Partitions on Plywood Floors."* American Plywood Association. Tacoma, WA.

drywall (see Figure 4.6). Blocking that is precut to the proper length for this purpose will contribute to convenience and accuracy.

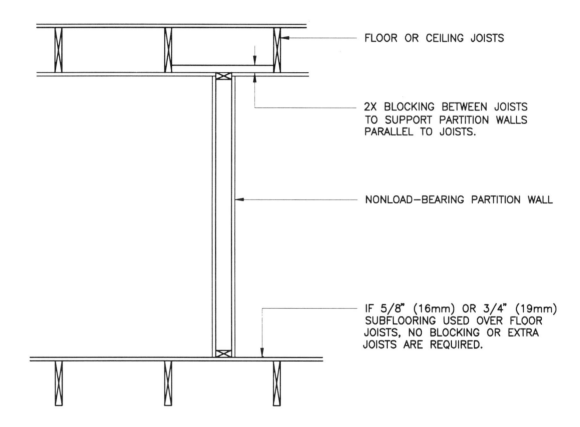

FLOOR OR CEILING JOISTS

2X BLOCKING BETWEEN JOISTS TO SUPPORT PARTITION WALLS PARALLEL TO JOISTS.

NONLOAD–BEARING PARTITION WALL

IF 5/8" (16mm) OR 3/4" (19mm) SUBFLOORING USED OVER FLOOR JOISTS, NO BLOCKING OR EXTRA JOISTS ARE REQUIRED.

FIGURE 4.6 Blocking for Nonload-Bearing Partitions

CHAPTER 5
EXTERIOR WALL CONSTRUCTION

Most homes built in the United States have exterior walls framed with wood studs. The conventional wood-frame wall is essentially an efficient construction, but its full potential is not often realized.

There are many opportunities to reduce both the material and labor costs in conventional wood-frame walls. This chapter discusses the application of cost-effective techniques to exterior wall framing, including studs, plates, and headers, as well as related elements (i.e., siding, windows, and doors). A 24-inch (610 mm) on-center stud spacing is suggested to coordinate with the 2-foot (610 mm) planning module discussed in Chapter 2.

REDUCED WALL HEIGHT

A rough wall height of slightly over 8 feet (2.44 m) is generally used in conventional homes to produce an 8-foot (2.44 m) ceiling height after installation of floor and ceiling finish materials. A full 8-foot-high (2.44 m) ceiling is not necessarily required, however. Building codes generally accept a 7-foot 6-inch (2.29 m) finished ceiling height for habitable rooms and a 7-foot (2.13 m) ceiling height for kitchens, bathrooms, and hallways. Research demonstrates that occupants are not even aware of the lower ceiling height.

A 7-foot 6-inch (2.29 m) ceiling height offers several advantages compared to the standard 8-foot (2.44 m) height. The lower wall height reduces the amount of material required for studs, insulation, and siding. It simplifies construction as workers can more readily reach that height for framing and finishing work. A 7-foot 6-inch (2.29 m) ceiling height often eliminates one tread in the stairs in two-story construction, thereby reducing the total run (length) of the stairs and providing more room to locate stairways. In addition, the lower ceiling height tends to increase the apparent room size on the interior and enhances the exterior profile, because the scale of the horizontal to vertical dimensions is greater, a factor that is especially significant in smaller homes.

Assuming a 1-1/2-inch-thick (38 mm) top and bottom plate, a nominal 7-foot 6-inch (2.29 m) finished ceiling height with a 7-foot 7-inch (2.31 m) rough dimension results in a stud length of 7 feet 4 inches (2.24 m). The shorter stud will have a lower compression stress. With 2-foot (610 mm) modular stud spacing, the reduced stud size is an important factor in engineering design.

TOP AND BOTTOM PLATES

Where all floor, wall, and roof framing members are aligned vertically and are coordinated on a 16- or 24-inch (406 or 610 mm) module, building loads are transmitted directly downward through roof rafters or trusses, studs, and floor joists. Top plates no longer serve as a structural beam to distribute concentrated loads from roof rafters or trusses to nonaligned studs. Similarly, bottom wall plates no longer distribute concentrated loads from studs to floor joists.

Wall plates of some sort are still a practical necessity for the layout, assembly, and erection of wall panels and for the attachment of wall panels to the floor and roof structure. They are also required for the wall panels to adequately develop shear strength. However, the traditional doubled 2x4 top plate is not required when framing members are aligned. Where roof rafters or trusses are aligned over studs, a single top plate is adequate to provide for attachment of the rafters or trusses. Generally, it is not a structural necessity to tie top plates at corners and other wall intersections. The reason is that attachments between the studs, sheathing, siding, and the roof system provide sufficient structural connection. In high-wind and seismic areas, however, metal plates or ties are recommended at these intersections.

It is beneficial to assemble wall sections—including framing and sheathing (if used) as well as siding, windows, and exterior trim—to the greatest extent possible before erection. This may be accomplished by using shop-fabricated wall panels or field fabricating walls horizontally on the floor deck. This type of tilt-up wall construction reduces construction time and labor.

WALL STUDS

As discussed previously, a modular layout is encouraged for floor, wall, and roof framing so that each member transmits its load directly to the next framing member below. Although 16-inch (406 mm) stud spacing has been more common in the past, building codes generally permit conventional 2x4 studs to be spaced up to 24 inches (610 mm) on center in single-story homes and in the second story of two-story homes. Some codes also permit 2x4 studs to be spaced 24 inches (610 mm) on center in the first story of two-story homes. In 1989, the Forest Products Laboratory of the U. S. Department of Agriculture stated in a publication that the strength of walls analyzed with 2x4 studs spaced 24 inches (610 mm) on center exceeded the maximum wind loadings that light-frame walls experience.[1] Even so, the building official may require engineering calculations to substantiate the use of 2x4 studs spaced 2 feet (610 mm) on center in any particular application.

Conventional engineering procedures for determining the load-carrying capacity of wood-frame walls are generally based on the structural skeleton alone. The only contribution normally credited to exterior and interior coverings is prevention of sideways buckling of the studs (shear strength). However, the Research Center has demonstrated that interior and exterior coverings

---

[1]*Light-Frame Wall and Floor Systems, Analysis and Performance.* U. S. Department of Agriculture Forest Service, Forest Products Laboratory, Washington, DC. 1989.

(such as gypsum drywall and fiberboard sheathing) can contribute to the strength and stiffness of wood-frame walls. A conservative design procedure was developed to allow for one-half the contribution of wall sheathing materials. This engineering procedure was used to check the adequacy of 2x4s spaced 24 inches (610 mm) on center with structural sheathing on the exterior and 1/2-inch (13 mm) gypsum wallboard on the interior. The section properties of the 2x4 material in this design were increased by

- multiplying the moment of inertia (I) by 1.50;
- multiplying the section modulus (S) by 1.25; and
- multiplying the area (A) by 1.05.

Although 2x3 studs are not commonly used for load-bearing walls in conventional building, they are structurally adequate where design loads are not excessive. The Research Center has demonstrated that exterior load-bearing walls with 7-foot 4-inch-long (2.24 m) 2x3 studs spaced at 2 feet (610 mm) on center are adequate for exterior load-bearing walls in single-story homes or the second story of two-story homes where

- house depth does not exceed 28 feet (8.53 m);
- design wind load does not exceed 15 psf (718 Pa);
- design snow load does not exceed 20 psf (958 Pa);
- allowable bending stress (F_b) of 2x3 material is at least 800 psi (5.52 MPa); and
- both exterior and interior surfaces are covered with 4x8 panel materials such as gypsum board, fiberboard sheathing, or their structural equivalents.

In recent years, builders have increased insulation levels in response to consumer demand for energy efficiency. Attics and basements usually have ample room to accommodate additional layers of insulation. In exterior walls, however, conventional 2x4 studs allow for only 3-1/2 inches (89 mm) of insulation. One of the most cost-effective solutions is to use 2x6 studs that allow room for 5-1/2 inches (140 mm) of insulation. Coincidently, the greater strength of 2x6 studs allows 24-inch (610 mm) on-center spacing for almost any design condition encountered in house building.

The most critical factor in designing wood studs is usually the horizontal wind load. For most types of residential construction, the wind pressure on exposed vertical surfaces ranges from 15 to 25 psf (718 to 1197 Pa), except in areas subject to more severe wind conditions (see Appendix C). In such cases, it may be more cost-effective to use 2x6 studs spaced 24 inches (610 mm) on center rather than 2x4 studs spaced 16 inches (406 mm) on center.

EXTERIOR WALL CORNERS

Though generally not dictated by structural considerations, conventional practice calls for a three-stud "corner post" at exterior wall corners. The third member serves primarily as a backer for the interior wall facing, usually 1/2-inch-thick (13 mm) gypsum drywall.

With the exception of high wind areas and Seismic Zones 3 and 4, the maximum load on the corner is approximately one-half the load on a regular stud, therefore, two-stud corners are more than adequate. The corner may be formed from the end studs in each of the two wall panels that meet at the corner. They are simply nailed together in conventional fashion as the wall panels are erected. No other special attachment is required at the typical corner.

Figure 5.1 depicts an alternative method of providing drywall back-up at corners with metal drywall "clips" spaced up to 2 feet (610 mm) apart. Clips of this type are preferred for ease of installation in areas of limited access. They are available from building hardware suppliers. Another alternative consists of a 1x3 lumber strip nailed to the back of the inside corner stud; however, the 1x3 must be nailed in place before the walls are covered on the exterior.

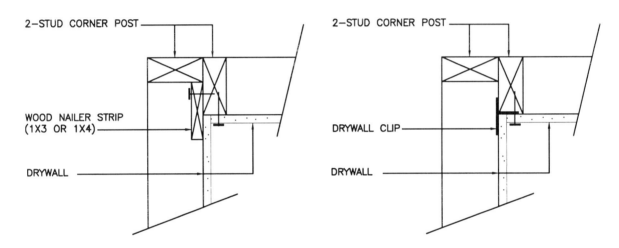

FIGURE 5.1 Alternative Methods for Providing Drywall Back-Up with a 2-Stud "Corner Post"

It should be noted that gypsum board is not actually fastened to the metal clips or wood backers. The sheet resting against the backers is installed first so that the second sheet, which is nailed to the stud, will lock the first in place. This provides a "floating joint," which is recommended to reduce cracking at the corners. It should also be noted that the two-stud corner is an energy saver since wall insulation can be installed in the space normally occupied by the third stud and the blocking.

PARTITION POSTS

Similar to corner posts, a two-stud "partition post" need not be built into the exterior wall for attachment of partitions. Except where a partition post is part of an engineered design, there is no structural requirement for anchorage of partitions to the exterior wall. Partitions that intersect the exterior wall at a normal stud location may be nailed directly to the exterior wall stud. Where partitions fall between normal stud locations, it is a good idea to install a mid-height block between the exterior wall studs to accommodate attachment of the end partition stud. The blocks should be installed flat-wise to allow insulation behind them. Back-up support for drywall at the intersection may be provided by metal clips or lumber strips as described for exterior wall corners.

MID-HEIGHT BLOCKING

As many who install blown-in insulation can testify, blocking between studs at approximately 4 feet (1.22 m) above the floor was common in older homes. However, such "fire" blocking is not necessary with platform framing, which is now standard practice. It is not necessary for either structural or fire safety reasons, and the major model building codes do not require such blocking. Wall studs are adequately braced by normal wall coverings, and top and bottom plates act as fire stops with platform framing.

DOOR AND WINDOW OPENINGS

Special care should be taken with door and window framing to ensure accurate, plumb, and square openings. Wherever possible, the location of door and window openings should be coordinated with a stud location on at least one side. This will simplify construction and eliminate at least one extra stud at each opening. Better yet, use modular window sizes that coordinate with a stud location on both sides so that no extra studs are required.

Where there are no floor or roof loads to be carried over an opening, there is no reason to use a header or supporting "jack" studs. The end walls of houses are typically nonload-bearing, assuming that overhead roof or floor framing bears on front and rear walls. Thus, structural headers are not required over door and window openings in exterior nonload-bearing walls. The openings may be single-framed with one stud at each side and a single stud-size member across the head.

Structural headers are, however, required to carry roof or floor loads over an opening in a load-bearing wall. However, where architectural design allows the use of windows with a 16-inch (406 mm) or 24-inch (610 mm) modular width, windows can be located between studs. Because all studs remain intact, no headers are required, even in load-bearing walls.

Floor design loads were described in Chapter 4. Typically, a 10 psf (479 Pa) dead load is assumed with either a 30 psf (1.44 kPa) or 40 psf (1.92 kPa) live load, depending on the local building code. The total roof design load consists of the dead load or weight of the structure itself plus the live load or snow load. The dead load of the roof/ceiling usually ranges between 10 and 15 psf (479 and 718 Pa) depending on the particular construction and combination of materials. Appendix C shows typical snow loads for different regions of the country.

It is important to examine the design loads before choosing a header. Figure 5.2 depicts several different roof and floor load combinations. When a window or door opening is directly beneath an opening in the story above, the lower header may be carrying floor loads only. Therefore, it is advantageous to align openings vertically in multistory construction to minimize header loads in the lower story. A single jack stud supporting each end of the header is usually adequate for spans less than 6 feet (1.83 m).

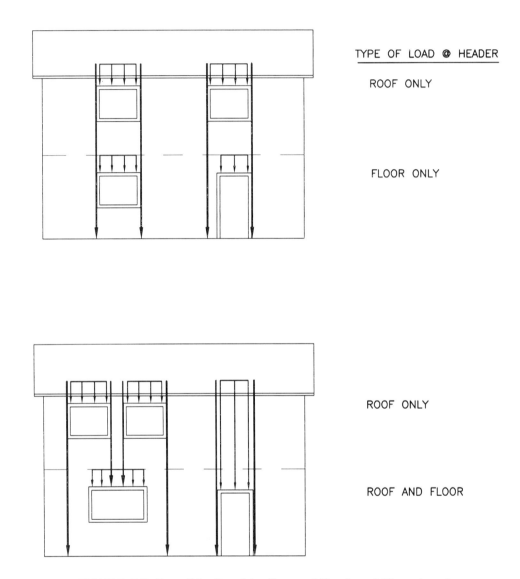

TYPE OF LOAD @ HEADER

ROOF ONLY

FLOOR ONLY

ROOF ONLY

ROOF AND FLOOR

**FIGURE 5.2 Possible Combinations of Roof and Floor Loads
Acting on Different Headers in a Two-Story Structure**

Lumber Headers

Conventionally, double 2x lumber headers are installed immediately above the wall opening with short "cripples" (abbreviated studs) installed between the header and top plate. An alternative is to install the header directly beneath the top plate and install a block across the top at the required opening height. With a nominal 7-foot 6-inch (2.29 m) wall height, a 2x8 header provides the correct opening height without any cripples or blocking (see Figure 5.3).

A greater effective window width can be created with a relatively small header size by placing two or more individual window units adjacent to each other. The header should be continuous across the adjacent openings, with intermediate jack studs installed between units to act as load-bearing mullions as shown in Figure 5.3. It is not necessary to shim and nail the two members of the header together. Further, where loads and span conditions permit, a single header may be used (see Figure 5.4). Table 5.1 and Figure 5.5 presents the allowable spans for conventional lumber headers with different roof and floor load conditions.

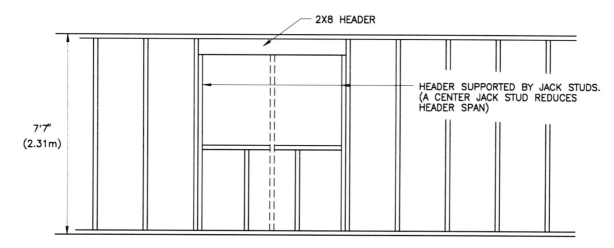

FIGURE 5.3 2x8 Header Installed Below Top Plate in Nominal 7-Foot 6-Inch Wall Continuous Across Adjacent Openings

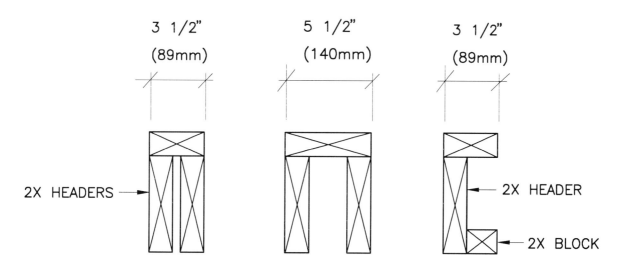

FIGURE 5.4 Single and Double Headers

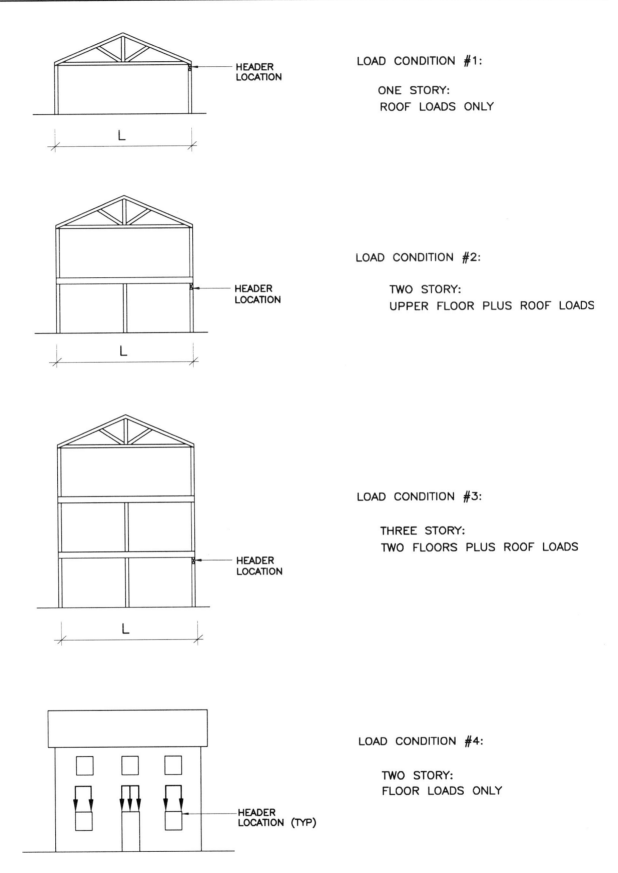

FIGURE 5.5 Load Conditions for Table 5.1

TABLE 5.1
Maximum Header Spans
based on house width and load condition (see Figure 5.5)

LOAD CONDITION	HEADER SIZE	HOUSE WIDTH									
		24 ft	7.32 m	26 ft	7.92 m	28 ft	8.53 m	30 ft	9.14 m	32 ft	9.75 m
		ft-in	meters	ft-in	meters	ft-in	meters	ft-in	meters	ft-in	meters
1 Roof Only	2- 2x3	2-1	0.63	2-0	0.61	—	—	—	—	—	—
	2- 2x4	2-11	0.89	2-10	0.85	2-8	0.82	2-7	0.79	2-6	0.77
	1- 2x6	3-3	0.99	3-1	0.95	3-0	0.91	2-11	0.88	2-10	0.86
	1- 2x8	4-3	1.30	4-1	1.25	4-0	1.21	3-10	1.16	3-8	1.13
	2- 2x6	4-7	1.40	4-5	1.34	4-3	1.29	4-1	1.25	4-0	1.21
	1- 2x10	5-5	1.66	5-3	1.60	5-1	1.54	4-11	1.49	4-9	1.44
	2- 2x8	6-0	1.84	5-10	1.77	5-7	1.70	5-5	1.65	5-3	1.59
	1- 2x12	6-8	2.02	6-4	1.94	6-2	1.87	5-11	1.81	5-9	1.75
	2- 2x10	7-9	2.35	7-5	2.26	7-2	2.18	6-11	2.10	6-8	2.03
	2- 2x12	9-4	2.86	9-0	2.75	8-8	2.65	8-5	2.56	8-1	2.47
2 Roof, Second Story Floor and Wall	2- 2x4	2-2	0.67	2-1	0.65	2-1	0.63	—	—	—	—
	1- 2x6	2-5	0.75	2-4	0.72	2-3	0.69	2-3	0.67	2-2	0.65
	1- 2x8	3-3	0.98	3-1	0.95	3-0	0.92	2-11	0.89	2-10	0.86
	2- 2x6	3-6	1.06	3-4	1.02	3-3	0.98	3-1	0.95	3-0	0.92
	1- 2x10	4-1	1.26	4-0	1.21	3-10	1.17	3-9	1.13	3-7	1.10
	2- 2x8	4-7	1.39	4-5	1.34	4-3	1.30	4-1	1.25	4-0	1.22
	1- 2x12	5-0	1.53	4-10	1.47	4-8	1.42	4-6	1.38	4-5	1.33
	2- 2x10	5-10	1.78	5-7	1.71	5-5	1.65	5-3	1.60	5-1	1.55
	2- 2x12	7-1	2.16	6-10	2.08	6-7	2.01	6-5	1.95	6-2	1.89
3 Roof, Second and Third Story Floors and Walls	1- 2x6	2-1	0.64	2-0	0.62	—	—	—	—	—	—
	1- 2x8	2-9	0.84	2-8	0.82	2-7	0.79	2-6	0.76	2-5	0.74
	2- 2x6	3-0	0.91	2-10	0.87	2-9	0.85	2-8	0.82	2-7	0.80
	1- 2x10	3-6	1.08	3-5	1.04	3-4	1.01	3-2	0.97	3-1	0.95
	2- 2x8	3-11	1.19	3-9	1.15	3-8	1.11	3-6	1.08	3-5	1.05
	1- 2x12	4-4	1.31	4-2	1.26	4-0	1.22	3-11	1.19	3-9	1.15
	2- 2x10	5-0	1.52	4-10	1.47	4-8	1.42	4-6	1.38	4-5	1.34
	2- 2x12	6-1	1.85	5-10	1.79	5-8	1.73	5-6	1.68	5-4	1.63
4 Second Story Floor Only	2- 2x3	2-8	0.80	2-6	0.77	2-5	0.74	2-4	0.72	2-3	0.70
	2- 2x4	3-8	1.12	3-6	1.08	3-5	1.04	3-4	1.01	3-2	0.97
	1- 2x6	4-1	1.25	3-11	1.20	3-9	1.16	3-8	1.12	3-7	1.08
	1- 2x8	5-5	1.65	5-2	1.58	5-0	1.52	4-10	1.47	4-8	1.43
	2- 2x6	5-10	1.77	5-7	1.70	5-4	1.64	5-2	1.58	5-0	1.53
	1- 2x10	6-11	2.10	6-7	2.02	6-5	1.95	6-2	1.88	6-0	1.82
	2- 2x8	7-8	2.33	7-4	2.24	7-1	2.16	6-10	2.08	6-7	2.02
	1- 2x12	8-5	2.56	8-1	2.46	7-9	2.37	7-6	2.29	7-3	2.21
	2- 2x10	9-9	2.97	9-4	2.86	9-0	2.75	8-9	2.66	8-5	2.57
	2- 2x12	11-10	3.61	11-5	3.47	11-0	3.35	10-7	3.23	10-3	3.13

Notes: End splits may not exceed one times the header depth.
For design load conditions (see Figure 5.5).
Minimum allowable bending stress F_b = 1000 psi (6895 kPa).

Glue-Nailed Plywood Box Headers

A structural header may also be formed by glue-nailing a plywood skin to framing members above the openings in a load-bearing wall. Plywood box headers use less material than conventional lumber headers and do not shrink as lumber headers often do. In addition, they are an energy saver because the cavity may be filled with insulation.

Figure 5.6 shows typical glue-nailed plywood headers. A single top plate is shown; this may be doubled, but at least one member must be continuous across the span. Jack studs are not normally required for spans of 4 feet (1.22 m) or less. The vertical "stiffeners" should be spaced the same as the studs (similar to cripple studs). The web may be installed to the inside and/or outside face with the face grain oriented horizontally. Table 5.2 provides allowable loads for different glue-nailed plywood headers. Additional information is available in *NAHB Research Report No. 5: Plywood Headers for Residential Construction.*[1]

The plywood thickness for either design should be a minimum of 1/2-inch (13 mm) and should be selected to blend with other wall covering materials. The plywood skins may be treated as sheathing or finished as an accent panel on the exterior, or they may be taped and spackled to blend with the drywall on the interior. A water-resistant structural adhesive should be used for gluing the plywood.

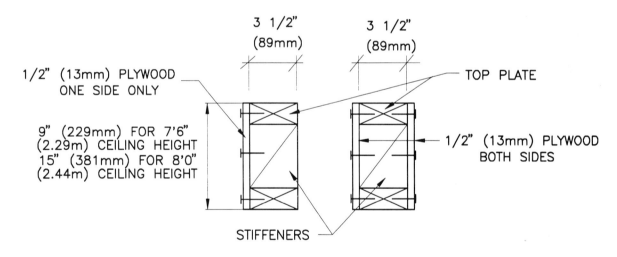

FIGURE 5.6 Glue-Nailed Box Headers

[1]*NAHB Research Report No. 5, Plywood Headers for Residential Construction.* NAHB Research Center. Prepared for the National Association of Home Builders, Washington, DC. 1983.

TABLE 5.2
Allowable Loads for Glue-Nailed Plywood Box Headers

HEADER TYPE	HEADER DEPTH		HEADER SPAN											
			3 ft.	0.91 m	4 ft.	1.22 m	5 ft.	1.52 m	6 ft.	1.83 m	7 ft.	2.13 m	8 ft.	2.44 m
	inches	mm	lb/ft	kN/m	lb/ft	kN/m	lb/ft	kN/m	lb/ft	kN/m	lb/ft	kN/m	lb/ft	kN/m
Plywood Both Sides	9	229	940	13.7	880	12.8	820	12.0	760	11.1	680	9.9	500	7.3
	15	381	1090	15.9	1040	15.2	990	14.4	940	13.7	860	12.6	740	10.8
Plywood on One Side	9	229	840	12.3	750	10.9	640	9.3	540	7.9	420	6.1	250	3.6
	15	381	900	13.1	810	11.8	720	10.5	650	9.5	580	8.5	520	7.6

Notes: 1.   Jack studs not required for spans of 4 feet (1.22 m) or less.
2.   2x4 minimum framing size, maximum stud spacing 24 inches (610 mm) on center.
3.   Plywood webs must be single piece with face grain parallel to span, minimum 1/2-inch (13 mm) structural rated plywood.
4.   Stiffener spacing is the same as basic stud spacing.
5.   Apply ¼-inch (6 mm) bead 3M wood adhesive (No. 5230) or equivalent to all framing under plywood webs, including stiffeners.   Nail with 8d common wire nails spaced 6 inches (152 mm) on center on all framing.   Insulate before enclosing.

Ref: *NAHB Research Report No. 5, Plywood Headers for Residential Construction.*   NAHB Research Center.   Prepared for the National Association of Home Builders, Washington, DC.   1983.

Window Opening Between Studs

Where compatible with architectural design, the use of nominal 22-1/2- or 14-1/2-inch-wide (572 or 368 mm) windows can simplify construction when such windows are located between regular studs. Blocks are installed at the proper heights for the head and sill and thus form the opening. Because no studs are displaced, this type of opening may be used in either load-bearing or nonload-bearing walls without requiring a structural header or jack studs.

Where a more expansive window width is desired, two or more adjacent stud spaces may be used in this manner to form a multiple-width opening. In this application, regular studs remain in place between individual units to function as load-bearing mullions (see Figure 5.7).

EXTERIOR SIDING/SHEATHING

A wide variety of siding products is available. Where used, structural siding panels installed directly to studs combine the functions of siding, sheathing, and structural bracing in a single layer. However, most siding products require some type of sheathing material for back-up support. The sheathing may also provide the required structural bracing for resisting wind and earthquake loads (check your local code).

Three-eighths-inch-thick (10 mm) wood structural panel sheathing provides good bracing strength in conventional construction as well as back-up for siding. Medium-density 1/2-inch-thick (13 mm) fiberboard sheathing also serves these functions. Other sheathing products rated for wall bracing are available. In combination with the gypsum drywall, these panels provide a rigid "system," however, in high wind and seismic areas the sheathing systems need to be properly designed.

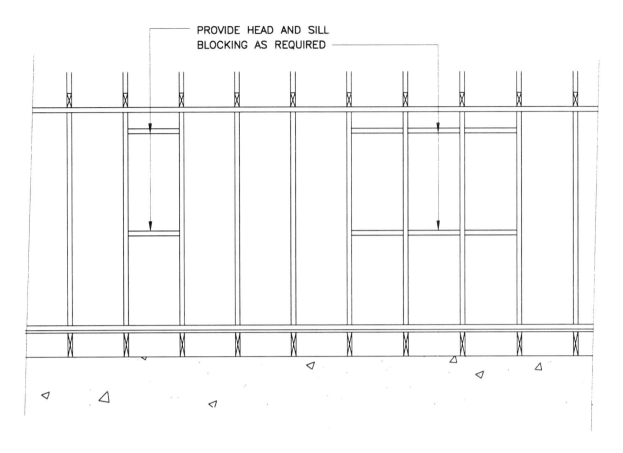

FIGURE 5.7 Single and Multiple Window Openings Between Studs

Some siding materials such as wood lap siding may be applied directly to studs but do not provide adequate bracing strength. Likewise, some sheathing materials such as plastic foam boards do not provide adequate bracing. In such cases, several alternative methods are available for providing the necessary bracing strength to exterior walls. Let-in 1x4 diagonal corner bracing is the traditional method. Metal angle or "T" braces that require only a saw cut to "let-in" one side of the angle or "T" are also available. Let-in bracing of any type is not permissible with 2x3 studs. Metal straps are also available for bracing that does not require letting-in. The straps must be installed diagonally in both directions to provide the required strength since they act only in tension. One 4-foot (1.22 m) wall section should be braced at each end and at intervals not to exceed 25 feet (7.62 m). In Seismic Zones 3 and 4 (see Appendix C), check with the local code official for additional requirements.

To simplify construction, the sheathing and/or siding should be applied to the wall framing before the wall panel is tilted up. Wall jacks are available where completed walls are too heavy to lift manually. Almost any siding product can be installed in this manner, especially on full-length walls. Regardless of the type of siding selected, a prefinished product saves on-site labor time and contributes to quality control. Most types of siding are available prefinished or at least preprimed.

EXTERIOR DOOR UNITS

Exterior doors provide for access into the home and control weather, privacy, and security. They may also contribute to light and ventilation. Generally, prehung door units are preferred as a means of simplifying construction and ensuring quality installation.

Insulated steel doors have gained a reputation for their stability, weathertightness, and generally trouble-free operation and service. Steel doors are commonly prehung in a wood-frame; both weatherstripping and the threshold are preinstalled. When prehung doors are used, storm doors are usually not cost-effective in terms of energy conservation.

WINDOW UNITS

Window units come in many different shapes and styles with a range of thermal values. Lower-priced windows generally have higher rates of air infiltration and lead to substantially more energy consumption over the life of the house. Most windows today—whether wood, plastic, or metal—are supplied prefinished on the exterior side. This provides a superior finish and eliminates a troublesome task near the end of the project.

Even the best windows will not perform satisfactorily if they are not installed properly. Although window units are commonly squared and braced before shipping, they may be distorted in transit and therefore should always be checked for squareness during installation. As with sheathing, window units may be installed before the wall is erected, especially if subsequent installation would require ladders or scaffolds and thus complicate the job.

The window frame should be fastened securely in the rough opening. Any shims should be installed carefully to avoid distorting the frame. Where drip caps and flashing are required, they should be installed with care to prevent water leakage. The entire unit should be well caulked at the joint between the exterior trim and the siding. The space between the window and rough frame should be filled with fiber insulation or foam caulk.

EXTERIOR TRIM AND FINISH

Exterior trim around doors, windows, corners, and other critical points serves an important purpose. Aside from appearance, the primary function of exterior trim is to cover construction joints and to help keep out wind and water. Properly placed exterior trim also provides needed construction tolerances.

Many architectural styles lend themselves to natural or rustic materials on the exterior, thereby permitting the use of less expensive lumber for trim. A rough-sawn surface, knots, and other natural characteristics can become an asset rather than a reflection of quality. Molded plastic architectural details can also provide a great deal of effect relative to their cost.

A solid or semitransparent stain finish may be considered instead of conventional paint for wood siding and trim. Stains provide good coverage and are not subject to cracking and peeling as are many conventional paints. Usually one coat is sufficient, especially where saw-textured wood is used. The stain may be applied by brush, roller or spray either on site or off site. Freshly finished pieces, especially those with a saw-textured surface can usually be stacked after an initial surface drying.

Prefinished trim and other accessories are available with most prefinished siding products to cover normal trim requirements at windows and corners. Prefinished soffit and fascia products are also available. Where they are not available, the required trim items can be prefinished by the builder or by a local supplier off site. Accessories such as colored caulk and siding nails are widely available to complete the finish. With prefinished siding, exterior painting can be all but eliminated.

Corrosion-resistant nails should always be used with exterior siding and trim. Stainless steel, aluminum, or hot-dip galvanized nails are recommended for this use. Electroplated galvanized nails, plain painted nails, and resin-coated nails corrode and stain trim and siding within a short time.

CHAPTER 6
ROOF CONSTRUCTION

Residential roof framing usually consists of either conventional joists and rafters or roof trusses. Conventional framing consists of opposing rafters set to the desired roof pitch tied at the bottom to form a triangle, with ceiling joists that are supported on a center bearing wall. Roof trusses are pre-engineered and assembled by a truss fabricator and usually span the entire width of the house. Either conventional roof framing or trusses may be used with a 24- or 16-inch (610 or 406 mm) framing module.

While conventional roof framing may be labor-intensive, it provides clear-span attic space for storage or additional living area and allows more flexibility in building complicated roof designs. Roof trusses, on the other hand, are easier and faster to install and eliminate the need for interior load-bearing walls. Braced rafters are a cross between conventional framing and trusses. They use purlins and braces to transfer roof loads directly to interior load-bearing walls and allow the use of smaller rafters or greater spans.

An important consideration in roof design independent of the type of construction is the roof pitch and type. A 4/12 or 5/12 roof pitch ensures adequate drainage. Steeper pitches are more difficult and more dangerous to construct. Flatter pitches are more prone to water leaks and the accumulation of leaves. Many different roof types are used today; one of the most popular and simplest types is the gable roof. Figure 6.1 shows different types of roof designs.

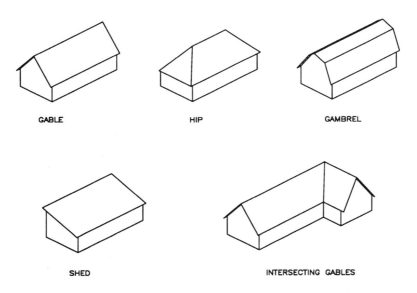

GABLE   HIP   GAMBREL

SHED   INTERSECTING GABLES

FIGURE 6.1 Roof Designs

CONVENTIONAL ROOF FRAMING

Conventional roof framing is an art that takes a degree of skill even for a simple roof. Roof rafters must be designed to carry the loads discussed in Chapter 3. Roof live load requirements vary with geographic location and local codes. A typical roof load may consist of a live (snow) load ranging from 10 to 60 psf (479 to 2873 kPa) and a dead load of 10 or 15 psf (479 or 718 kPa). Table 6.1 provides rafter tables for selected live loads; Appendix C includes snow and wind load maps.

Conventional rafters must be well secured to the ceiling joists so that the walls cannot be pushed out by the load on the roof. In addition, the rafters are typically braced with collar ties installed at the top one-third of the attic space and typically spaced 4 feet (1.22 m) apart. Figure 6.2 shows a typical rafter and ceiling joist system. Ceiling joists are designed by taking into consideration the dead load and live load for attic storage. Where attic storage is not allowed, the design live load is usually 10 psf (479 kPa) and the dead load is 5 psf (239 kPa). Where limited attic storage is allowed but development of future rooms is not possible, the design live load is usually 20 psf (958 kPa) and the dead load is 10 psf (479 kPa) (see Table 6.2).

Once the walls are built, plumbed, and braced, the roof can be framed. The exterior walls must be carefully aligned because any irregularities will become permanent once the roof is in place. With cost-effective construction, the rafters should line up with the wall studs. In fact, it may not even be necessary to mark rafter positions on the wall plate. Rafter positions also determine the location of the ceiling joists. For roofs in high-wind areas, rafters should be tied down to the walls with metal straps or anchors. The local building code should be consulted to determine if straps are needed and if so, the type and size required. Purlins or intermediate supports for rafters between the ridge and the wall are used in braced rafter construction to reduce rafter span and size. Figure 6.3 shows a braced rafter system. Allowable rafter spans may be taken from Table 6.1.

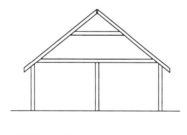

RAFTERS WITH RIDGE BOARD,
CEILING JOISTS, AND COLLAR TIES

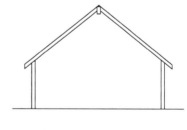

CATHEDRAL CEILING WITH
RIDGE BEAM

FIGURE 6.2 Conventional Joist and Rafter Construction

TABLE 6.1
Allowable Spans for Roof Rafters

RAFTER			DESIGN VALUE IN BENDING							
SIZE	SPACING		800 psi	5516 kPa	1000 psi	6895 kPa	1200 psi	8274 kPa	1400 psi	9653 kPa
	inches	mm	ft-in	m	ft-in	m	ft-in	m	ft-in	m
20 psf (958 Pa) LIVE LOAD										
2x6	16	406	10-0	3.05	11-3	3.43	12-4	3.76	13-3	4.04
	24	610	8-2	2.49	9-2	2.79	10-0	3.05	10-10	3.30
2x8	16	406	13-3	4.04	14-10	4.52	16-3	4.95	17-6	5.33
	24	610	10-10	3.30	12-1	3.68	13-3	4.04	14-4	4.37
2x10	16	406	16-11	5.16	18-11	5.77	20-8	6.30	22-4	6.81
	24	610	13-9	4.19	15-5	4.70	16-11	5.16	18-3	5.56
E-10⁶ psi/ kPa	16	406	0.58	4.00	0.82	5.65	1.07	7.38	1.35	9.31
	24	610	0.48	3.31	0.67	4.62	0.88	6.07	1.10	7.58
30 psf (1435 Pa) LIVE LOAD										
2x6	16	406	8-8	2.64	9-9	2.97	10-8	3.25	11-6	3.51
	24	610	7-1	2.16	7-11	2.41	8-8	2.64	9-5	2.87
2x8	16	406	11-6	3.51	12-10	3.91	14-0	4.27	15-2	4.62
	24	610	9-4	2.84	10-6	3.20	11-6	3.51	12-5	3.78
2x10	16	406	14-8	4.47	16-4	4.98	17-11	5.46	19-4	5.89
	24	610	11-11	3.63	13-4	4.06	14-8	4.47	15-10	4.83
E-10⁶ psi/ kPa	16	406	0.57	3.93	0.80	5.52	1.05	7.24	1.32	9.10
	24	610	0.46	3.17	0.65	4.48	0.85	5.86	1.08	7.45
40 psf (1915 Pa) LIVE LOAD										
2x6	16	406	7-9	2.36	8-8	2.64	9-6	2.90	10-3	3.12
	24	610	6-4	1.93	7-1	7.08	7-9	2.36	8-5	2.57
2x8	16	406	10-3	3.12	11-6	3.51	12-7	3.84	13-7	4.14
	24	610	8-4	2.54	9-4	2.84	10-3	3.12	11-1	3.38
2x10	16	406	13-1	3.99	14-8	4.47	16-0	4.88	17-4	5.28
	24	610	10-8	3.25	11-11	3.63	13-1	3.99	14-2	4.32
E-10⁶ psi/ kPa	16	406	0.54	3.72	0.76	5.24	1.00	6.89	1.26	8.69
	24	610	0.44	3.03	0.62	4.27	0.81	5.58	1.03	7.10
50 psf (2394 Pa) LIVE LOAD										
2x6	16	406	7-1	2.16	7-11	2.41	8-8	2.64	9-5	2.87
	24	610	5-10	1.78	6-6	1.98	7-1	2.16	7-8	2.34
2x8	16	406	9-4	2.84	10-6	3.20	11-6	3.51	12-5	3.78
	24	610	7-8	2.34	8-7	2.62	9-4	2.84	10-1	3.07
2x10	16	406	11-11	3.63	13-4	4.06	14-8	4.47	15-10	4.83
	24	610	9-9	2.97	10-11	3.33	11-11	3.63	12-11	3.94
E-10⁶ psi/ kPa	16	406	0.52	3.59	0.72	4.96	0.95	6.55	1.20	8.27
	24	610	0.42	2.90	0.59	4.07	0.77	5.31	0.98	6.76

Notes:
1. Live load plus dead load of 10 psf (479 Pa) determines the required bending design value.
2. The modulus of elasticity, E, in 1,000,000 psi (kPa) is shown at the bottom of each table.
3. Allowable spans are based on a deflection of L/240 at design load.

Ref: *Span Tables for Joists and Rafters.* American Forest & Paper Association, Washington, DC. 1993. Used by permission of AFPA.

TABLE 6.2
Allowable Spans for Ceiling Joists

JOIST			MODULUS OF ELASTICITY, E, in 1,000,000 psi or kPa							
SIZE	SPACING		1.0 psi	6.89 kPa	1.2 psi	8.27 kPa	1.40 psi	9.65 kPa	1.60 psi	11.03 kPa
	inches	mm	ft-in	m	ft-in	m	ft-in	m	ft-in	m
10 psf (479 Pa) LIVE LOAD (no attic storage)										
2x4	16	406	9-8	2.95	10-3	3.12	10-9	3.28	11-3	3.43
	24	610	8-5	2.57	8-11	2.72	9-5	2.87	9-10	3.00
2x6	16	406	15-2	4.62	16-1	4.90	16-11	5.16	17-8	5.38
	24	610	13-3	4.04	14-1	4.29	14-9	4.50	15-6	4.72
2x8	16	406	19-11	6.07	21-2	6.45	22-4	6.81	23-4	7.11
	24	610	17-5	5.31	18-6	5.64	19-6	5.94	20-5	6.22
2x10	16	406	25-5	7.75	--	--	--	--	--	--
	24	610	22-3	6.78	23-8	7.21	24-10	7.57	26-0	7.92
F_b-psi/ kPa	16	406	909	6267	1026	7074	1137	7839	1243	8570
	24	610	1040	7171	1174	8094	1302	8977	1423	9811
20 psf (958 Pa) LIVE LOAD (limited attic storage)										
2x4	16	406	7-8	2.34	8-1	2.46	8-7	2.62	8-11	2.72
	24	610	6-8	2.03	7-1	2.16	7-6	2.29	7-10	2.39
2x6	16	406	12-0	3.66	12-9	3.89	13-5	4.09	14-1	4.29
	24	610	10-6	3.20	11-2	3.40	11-9	3.58	12-3	3.73
2x8	16	406	15-10	4.83	16-10	5.13	17-9	5.41	18-6	5.64
	24	610	13-10	4.22	14-8	4.47	15-6	4.72	16-2	4.93
2x10	16	406	20-2	6.15	21-6	6.55	22-7	6.88	23-8	7-21
	24	610	17-8	5.38	18-9	5.72	19-9	6.02	20-8	6.30
F_b-psi/ kPa	16	406	1145	7895	1293	8915	1433	9880	1566	10797
	24	610	1310	9032	1480	10204	1640	11307	1793	12362

Note: Allowable spans are based on a deflection of L/240 at design load.
   Dead load is 10 psf (479 Pa). The required bending design value, F_b, in psi or kPa is shown at the bottom of each section of the table.
Ref: *Span Tables for Joists and Rafters.* American Forest & Paper Association, Washington, DC. 1993. Used by permission of AFPA.

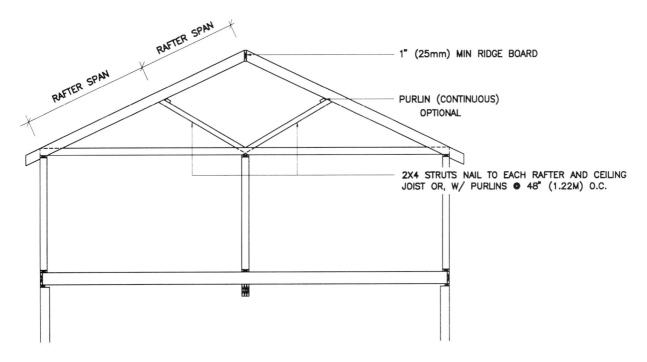

FIGURE 6.3 Braced Rafter System

ENGINEERED ROOF TRUSSES

Wood trusses are generally the most highly engineered component used in house construction today. They are widely accepted and are readily available in most areas. Requiring only basic carpentry skills, wood trusses are easy to install and provide a means of rapidly enclosing the building shell. Trusses adapt to most roof designs, including hips, L-shaped plans, and other variations. However, the most cost-effective design is a straight gable rectangular roof.

Trusses are normally designed for 24-inch (610 mm) on-center spacing, which integrates with the 2-foot (610 mm) planning module. When installed directly over wall studs, a single top plate on the wall provides ample anchorage by conventional toe-nailing under normal conditions. In high-wind regions (20 psf [958 Pa] or greater wind uplift), additional anchor straps may be required to tie trusses to wall studs. See wind map and table in Appendix C.

Several basic types of trusses are available depending on architectural and engineering design factors (see Figure 6.4). The "Fink" or "W" truss is the most widely used type. The arrangement of web members in a Fink truss is structurally efficient and allows good access through the center portion. The "Howe" truss is also structurally efficient, but the arrangement of web members tends to interfere with attic access.

Several variations of "scissors" truss designs are sometimes used to provide a "cathedral" ceiling. Scissors trusses may be mixed with standard trusses in the same roof system to provide a cathedral ceiling feature over a portion of the house.

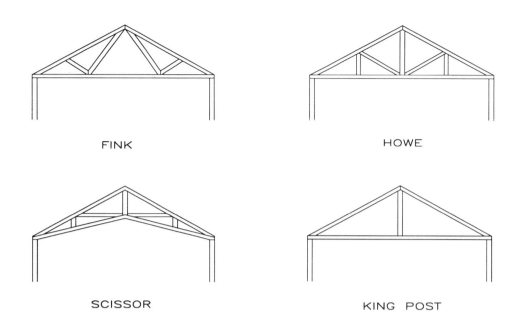

FINK

HOWE

SCISSOR

KING POST

FIGURE 6.4 Basic Roof Truss Designs

A simple "king post" truss provides a clean appearance, especially where the trusses are exposed. While truss manufacturers can design a king post truss to support the required design loads, the king post truss is not as efficient and the members are larger than those of a Fink or Howe truss.

Truss fabricators normally have the capability of supplying the necessary engineering for each unique design condition. It may be possible to specify the length of the top chord to a multiple of 2 feet (610 mm) to permit maximum use of truss lumber and roof sheathing material. Any excess length can usually be taken up in the roof overhang. Maximum spans for selected Fink, Howe, scissors, and king post truss types at 24-inch (610 mm) spacing are provided in Appendix G.

Prefabricated gable ends are generally available as part of the truss package. They resemble a truss but have vertical members spaced at 2 feet (610 mm) or 16 inches (406 mm) on center in lieu of truss web members. Therefore, they are not a true structural truss and should not be used over a clear span. Rough openings for attic vents are typically built into gable end trusses. Some fabricators also preapply sheathing as needed. Sheathing or siding is applied to the vertical members of the gable end truss just as it is installed to studs. Installation of gable end sheathing, siding, vents, and rake trim before erection can simplify the job.

Attachment of a 2x4 "flange" along the bottom chord is also recommended before erection (see Figure 6.5). The gable end is then installed by nailing down through the flange into the top plate of the wall. The flange also serves as back-up blocking for the drywall ceiling. Where a panel siding product is used on the gable end, a lap joint over the wall siding is recommended to provide an effective weathertight joint with ample field tolerance.

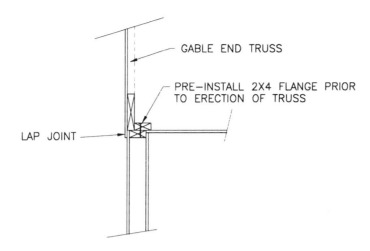

GABLE END TRUSS

PRE-INSTALL 2X4 FLANGE PRIOR
TO ERECTION OF TRUSS

LAP JOINT

FIGURE 6.5
2x4 Flange Along Bottom Chord of Gable End

Trusses are laterally unstable until the roof sheathing is installed. Accordingly, caution should be exercised during erection of the trusses, particularly with larger trusses, especially those taller than a man. The HIB-91 Summary Sheet published by the Truss Plate Institute[1] should be followed for handling, installing, and bracing trusses. Some of the recommendations in the publication include the following:

- Trusses should not be unloaded on rough terrain or uneven surfaces.
- Do not attach cables, chains, or hooks to the web members for lifting.
- Do not lift single trusses with spans greater than 30 feet (9.14 m) by the peak.
- All temporary bracing should be no less than 2x4 grade marked lumber.
- Besides lateral and diagonal temporary truss bracing, trusses should be braced to the ground and/or building interior (see Figure 6.6; for more details see the HIB-91 Summary sheet).
- Trusses should not be cut without consulting the truss manufacturer.
- Construction loads should not be placed on unbraced trusses.

For further information on roof or floor truss applications or metal-plate-connected wood truss design and construction, contact your local truss fabricator, the Wood Truss Council of America,[2] or the Truss Plate Institute.[3]

---

[1]*HIB-91 Summary Sheet.* Truss Plate Institute, Madison, WI. 1991. Courtesy of Truss Plate Institute.

[2]Wood Truss Council of America, 5937 Meadowwood Drive, Suite 14, Madison, WI 53711 4125.

[3]Truss Plate Institute, 583 D'Onofrio Drive, Suite 200, Madison, WI 53719.

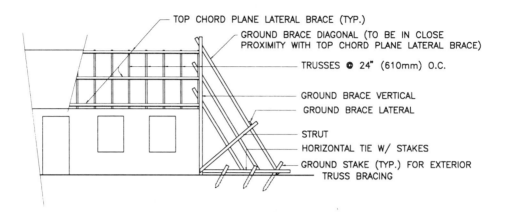

FIGURE 6.6 Roof Trusses Braced on the Building Exterior

ROOF SHEATHING

Roof sheathing may consist of wood structural panels such as oriented strandboard (OSB) or plywood. The key term is "structural" because the panels must be adequate to carry the roof live loads. Wood structural panels may also be rated by the American Plywood Association[1] (APA) as one of the following:

- APA Rated Sheathing Exposure 1 or 2;
- APA Rated Sheathing Exterior;
- APA Structural 1 Rated Sheathing Exposure 1; or
- APA Structural 1 Rated Sheathing Exterior.

Maximum spans for roof sheathing are given in Table 6.3. For example, the table indicates that, for a 24-inch (610 mm) truss or rafter spacing with a 30 psf (1.44 kPa) live load and edge support, 3/8-inch-thick (10 mm) roof sheathing is acceptable.

The long dimension or strength axis of the panel should be installed across the supports, with the panel running continuously over at least two spans. Suitable edge support may be provided between rafters or trusses, as indicated in Table 6.3, by the use of metal "H" clips (see Figure 6.7). Panel end joints should be located over framing members. A 1/8-inch (3 mm) spacing should be allowed at panel ends and edges. Panel end joints need not be staggered over alternate trusses, thereby simplifying roof sheathing layout and reducing the number of cuts required.

---

[1]*APA Design/Construction Guide: Residential and Commercial.* American Plywood Association, Tacoma, WA. 1993.

TABLE 6.3
Maximum Spans and Uniform Roof Live Loads for APA Rated Sheathing[1]
with long dimension perpendicular to supports

PANEL SPAN RATING[2]	MINIMUM NOMINAL PANEL THICKNESS		MAXIMUM SPAN				ALLOWABLE LIVE LOADS (psf, Pa)[4] SPACING OF SUPPORTS (CENTER TO CENTER)			
			WITH EDGE SUPPORT[3]		WITHOUT EDGE SUPPORT					
	in.	mm	in.	mm	in.	mm	16 in.	406 mm	24 in.	610 mm
16/0	5/16	8	16	406	16	406	30	1436	---	---
20/0	5/16	8	20	508	20	508	50	2394	---	---
24/0	3/8	10	24	610	20[5]	508	100	4788	30	1436
24/16	7/16	11	24	610	24	610	100	4788	40	1915
32/16	15/32	12	32	813	28	711	180	8618	70	3352
40/20	19/32	15	40	1016	32	813	305	14,603	130	6224
48/24	23/32	18	48	1219	36	914	---	---	175	8379
60/32	7/8	22	60	1524	48	1219	---	---	305	14,603

Notes:
1. APA rated sheathing with span rating indicated may be manufactured as plywood, a composite, or OSB that satisfies APA specifications. Includes APA rated sheathing/ceiling deck panels.
2. The numerator represents the allowable spans for roofs, the denominator represents the allowable spans for floors.
3. Tongue-and-groove edges, panel edge clips (one midway between each support, except two equally spaced between supports 48 inches [1.22 m] on center), lumber blocking, or other. For low-sloped roofs, see APA Table 22.
4. 10 psf (479 Pa) dead load assumed.
5. 24 inches (610 mm) for 15/32-inch (12 mm) and 1/2-inch (13 mm) panels.

Ref: *APA Design/Construction Guide*, Table 21. American Plywood Association, Tacoma, WA. 1993. Used by permission of APA.

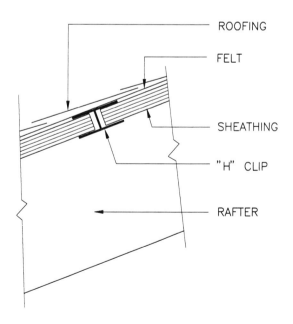

ROOFING

FELT

SHEATHING

"H" CLIP

RAFTER

FIGURE 6.7 Metal "H" Clips for Roof Sheathing

The roof sheathing should be securely fastened to the roof framing. Damage resulting from hurricanes such as Andrew (1992) and Iniki (1992) have prompted new roof sheathing fastening schedules. Figure 6.8 and Table 6.4 are based on fastening schedules proposed by the APA.

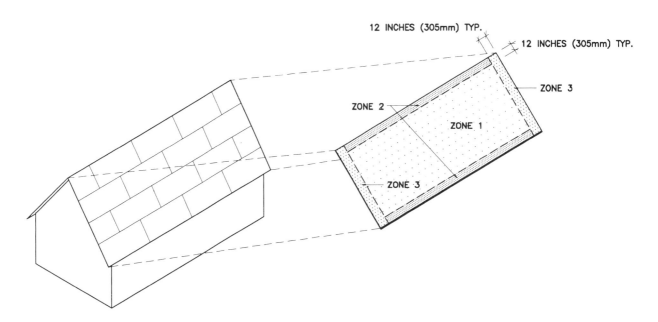

FIGURE 6.8 Diagram for Roof Sheathing Fastening Schedule

TABLE 6.4
Roof Sheathing Nail Spacing[1]
roof framing 24 inches (610 mm) on center, nominal panel thickness ≤ 5/8-inch (16 mm)

FASTENING ZONE (FROM FIG. 6.8)	LOCATION	BASIC WIND SPEED (APPENDIX C)					
		≤80 mph (129 kph)[2]		>80 mph (129 kph)[2]		≥90 mph (145 kph)[3]	
		inches	millimeters	inches	millimeters	inches	millimeters
1	Panel Ends and at Gable End Wall or Truss	6	152	6	152	6	152
	Intermediate Supports	12	305	12	305	6	152
2	Panel Ends and at Gable End Wall or Truss	6	152	6	152	6	152
	Intermediate Supports	12	305	6	152	6	152
3	Panel Ends and at Gable End Wall or Truss	6	152	4	102	4[4]	102
	Intermediate Supports	12	305	6	152	6[4]	152

Notes: 1. Use 3d common nails except as noted.
2. Basic wind speed; mean roof height ≤35 feet (10.7 m).
3. For lower density framing, windows breached. Basic wind speed; should be considered for hurricane oceanline (Atlantic Ocean and Gulf of Mexico coastal areas) and the transition zone between hurricane oceanline and inland areas, and those inland regions in which the basic wind speeds are greater than or equal to 90 mph; mean roof height ≤35 feet (10.7 m)
4. For a mean roof height greater than 25 feet (7.6 m) and less than or equal to 35 feet (10.7 m), use 8d ring-shank nails in Fastening Zone 3.

Ref: *APA Data File T325: Roof Sheathing Fastening Schedules for Wind Uplift.* American Plywood Association, Tacoma, WA. 1993. Used by permission of APA.

ATTIC VENTILATION

Ventilation of attic and roof/ceiling spaces helps lower air temperature in the summer and allows moisture vapor to escape in winter, minimizing the chance for damaging condensation. Good ventilation also helps prevent the formation of ice dams at the eave edge of the roof. Ice dams occur when melted snow freezes at the roof overhang. The resulting trapped water makes its way under the shingles and through the roof, ceiling, and walls.

Ventilation may be provided with the use of gable, ridge, soffit, or roof vents. End vents are usually the least expensive to install in gable roofs with attic space. Where a vapor barrier is provided in the ceiling, 1 square foot (929 mm²) of net free ventilating area should be provided for each 300 square feet (27.9 m²) of ceiling. Where no vapor barrier is provided, 1 square foot (929 mm²) of net free ventilating area should be provided for each 150 square feet (13.9 m²) of ceiling.[1] A vapor barrier is not recommended in cold climates where excessive moisture may be trapped in a tightly built house. Cross-ventilation may be provided by placing one-quarter of the specified area at each soffit and one-half at least 3 feet (914 mm) above the soffit. With this arrangement, the ventilating area may be reduced by one-half for gable roofs without a vapor barrier.

Cathedral ceilings are particularly vulnerable to condensation. At least a 2-inch (51 mm) space should be left between the insulation and roof sheathing. This space should be vented by soffit vents at the bottom and a ridge vent at the top. Warm air in the roof cavity rises to the ridge from both sides of the roof and escapes through the ridge vent. A vapor retarder is also recommended for cathedral ceilings.

Now that ceiling insulation practice typically calls for a 6-inch (152 mm) or greater thickness of insulation, special measures may be required to prevent the blocking of eave vents. One solution uses a cantilevered roof truss to provide added height above the outside wall (see Figure 6.9). The insulation can extend over the top plate of the wall and still allow a ventilation space between the insulation and the underside of the roof sheathing. Another solution is to install ventilation tunnels between trusses or rafters to provide a passageway for ventilation, particularly when loose-fill insulation is used.[2]

ROOF TRIM DETAILS

Traditional homes often have details that include a fascia, soffit, frieze, special moldings, etc. Detail work of this kind can add substantially to the cost of the house. Many of these details may be eliminated or simplified with no loss in function while still providing a finished appearance. The following suggestions can save roof trim and soffit costs.

---

[1]*Insulation Manual - Homes, Apartments.* NAHB Research Center, Upper Marlboro, MD. 1971.

[2]*Controlling Moisture in Homes.* National Association of Home Builders, Washington, DC. 1987.

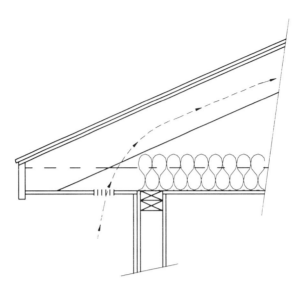

**FIGURE 6.9 Cantilevered Truss
Construction to Improve Ventilation**

As with other exterior trim, less expensive lumber may be used for rake and eave trim when the natural characteristics of the wood are treated as an architectural feature. Rough-sawn lumber is especially appropriate in this type of application, but it should be dry. A solid or semi-transparent stain finish may also be considered for rake and soffit trim as discussed in Chapter 5. It is generally advantageous to prefinish roof trim items either on or off site in order to reduce field labor and to avoid paint lines and runs on the siding. Color-matched 8d siding nails are well suited for applying trim, although unpainted casing head or finish nails may also be used. In either case, high-quality corrosion-resistant nails should be used.

Trim details at the rake edge of the roof are essentially nonfunctional. If gable end siding is fitted to the underside of roofing, rake trim may be entirely eliminated or limited to a metal drip edge. However, some trim may be desirable along the rake for appearance. A trim strip at this point also contributes to field tolerance by covering the rough edge of gable end siding. A simple rake board, anywhere from 1x2 to 1x6 in size, can conceal inaccuracies in fitting gable end siding and provide a more finished appearance.

A gable overhang is also essentially nonfunctional. However, where it is considered desirable, an open soffit detail may be created at minimal cost by simply extending the roof sheathing out over the gable end and attaching a "rake board" along the outer edge. A maximum 12-inch (305 mm) overhang is possible by using this method. A selected 2x4 or 2x6 of sufficient length may be used as a trim board as shown in Figure 6.10. Roofing nails that penetrate the exposed roof sheathing are not considered a problem where open soffits of this type are used. Nail tips are not readily noticeable in the shaded recess of the soffit, especially if a dark stain or paint is used in this area.

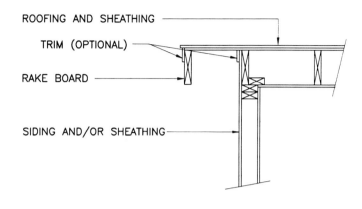

ROOFING AND SHEATHING

TRIM (OPTIONAL)

RAKE BOARD

SIDING AND/OR SHEATHING

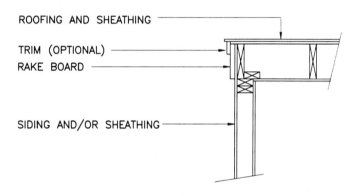

ROOFING AND SHEATHING

TRIM (OPTIONAL)
RAKE BOARD

SIDING AND/OR SHEATHING

FIGURE 6.10 Simplified Rake Trim Details

The primary function of the trim detail at the eave edge of a roof is to cover openings between roof framing members. If there is no overhang and the siding is extended upward to cover rafter or truss ends, eave trim may be entirely eliminated or limited to a metal drip edge. However, as with the rake detail, it may be desirable to provide some trim along the eave for appearance. Eave trim may be limited to a simple fascia board applied directly to the rafter or truss ends. A 1x6 or 1x8 fascia is usually sufficient depending on the size of the rafters or trusses used. Where there is no overhang, a gutter is recommended to prevent water from running down the sidewall. The gutter also becomes part of the trim detail at the eave (see Figure 6.11).

A soffit overhang is often considered desirable to protect the walls from rain and the windows from summer sun. Where an overhang is used, an inexpensive open soffit detail can eliminate much of the cost of a traditional "cornice." All trim details on the underside of the soffit may be eliminated, leaving the rafter or truss tails exposed (see Figure 6.12). Precut blocks can then be installed between the rafters or trusses. A 1x6 or 1x8 fascia installed across truss ends can support the roof sheathing and provide a finished appearance. Where thicker sheathing that does not require edge support (such as 1x6 boards) is used, the fascia board may be eliminated.

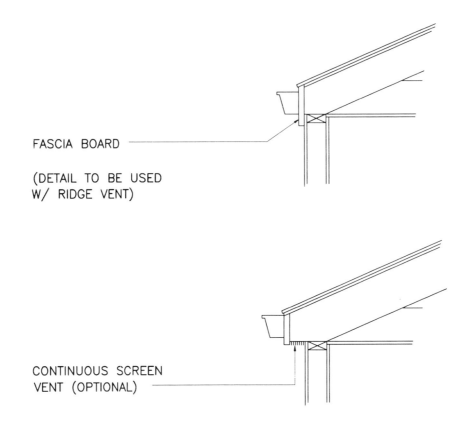

FASCIA BOARD

(DETAIL TO BE USED
W/ RIDGE VENT)

CONTINUOUS SCREEN
VENT (OPTIONAL)

FIGURE 6.11 Simplified Eave Details without Overhang

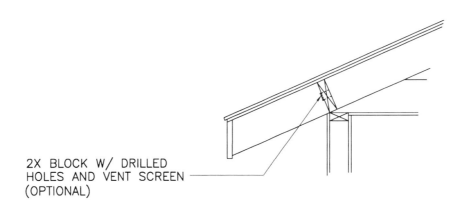

2X BLOCK W/ DRILLED
HOLES AND VENT SCREEN
(OPTIONAL)

FIGURE 6.12 Simplified Eave Details with Overhang

The amount of overhang may vary but should be selected with the type of roof construction and the need for summer shading in mind. It may be possible to adjust the overhang so that the length of the rafter or top chord is a multiple of 2 feet (610 mm). This will provide for efficient use of the rafter or truss material and the roof sheathing. Rafter or truss ends are usually plumb cut to provide for installation of a gutter, if required. However, a gutter is not always essential with an overhang of at least 12 inches (305 mm).

As noted previously, roofing nails that penetrate the exposed underside of roof sheathing do not necessarily present a problem. Nail tips are not readily visible in the shaded recess of the soffit, especially where a dark stain or paint is used. However, if a thicker sheathing material such as 1x6 boards is used in this area, roofing nails need not penetrate all the way through.

ROOF COVERING

Asphalt shingle roofing is the least expensive and most versatile roofing material available. It is highly tolerant to field conditions and does not require a high degree of skill to install. Asphalt shingles readily adapt to various roof design conditions, including eaves, ridges, hips, valleys, chimneys, vents, etc., with little waste. The typical life expectancy of standard 210-pound (934 N) asphalt shingles is 15 to 20 years depending on climate. Lighter colors reflect more heat and provide cooler roofs in warm climates. The self-sealing tabs provide extra protection against wind damage. However, standard asphalt roofing is not designed to withstand the high winds associated with hurricanes.

Wood structural sheathing should be covered as soon as possible to protect it from excessive exposure to moisture before application of the roofing material. Roofing felt may or may not be required depending on the length of time between the installation of the sheathing and the completion of the roofing. When roofing paper is used, it should be covered with shingles the same day or well nailed with large washer-head nails to resist the wind. Field experience suggests that such a roofing underlay is unnecessary in low- and moderate-wind areas when "seal-down" shingles are used with a roof pitch of 4/12 or greater. However, manufacturer's specifications should be followed. Roof slopes less than 3/12 are not recommended. Where used, they require special measures to protect against wind, water, and ice damage, and the roof covering manufacturer's recommendations should be followed.

CHAPTER 7
INTERIOR PARTITIONS AND FINISH

This chapter discusses cost-effective construction principles for nonload-bearing partition framing, interior surfaces, trim, and other finish items required to complete the interior of the house. Emphasis is placed on concepts that minimize costs by reducing, eliminating, and simplifying trim details wherever possible.

NONLOAD-BEARING PARTITION FRAMING

Interior load-bearing walls transmit floor and roof loads from above to the floor and underlying structure below. They are framed with essentially the same studs, plates, and headers as exterior load-bearing walls. In contrast, the primary function of nonload-bearing partitions is simply to divide interior space and provide a desirable degree of privacy.

Wood stud framing is widely used for partition construction because of its relative cost effectiveness. It is simple and efficient and requires no special procedures compared to other framing. Because structural requirements are minimal, the size of framing members may be smaller than for load-bearing walls, and the spacing may be greater.

The use of 2x3 studs spaced at 24 inches (610 mm) on center for nonload-bearing partitions is acceptable under virtually all building codes. It is more than adequate to meet performance requirements and has been well accepted wherever used. Occupants are generally unaware of and unconcerned with any difference compared to a traditional 2x4 wall. The usable floor area is increased by perhaps 12 to 14 square feet (1.11 to 1.30 m^2) in a typical home.

Because the studs in a nonload-bearing partition do not carry vertical loads, it is not necessary to coordinate their location with structural members in the floor or roof. Nonload-bearing partitions may be located wherever desired and need not bear over other framing members. Stud spacing is primarily a function of providing support to the facing material, usually gypsum drywall, and may be 2 feet (610 mm) on center starting from either end.

Normally, single 2x top and bottom plates are used in partitions. When used in conjunction with a 7-foot 7-inch (2.31 m) rough ceiling height, as previously discussed in Chapter 5, the net length of a partition stud with 2x plates is 7 feet 4 inches (2.24 m). It is also possible to use 1x plates for nonload-bearing partitions. When used with a 7-foot 7-inch (2.31 m) rough ceiling height, the net length of partition studs with 1x plates is 7 feet 5-1/2-inches (2.27 m).

Light-Gauge Steel Partitions

Light-gauge steel partition studs are commonly used in multifamily and light commercial construction, and offer an alternative in single-family homes. Steel studs have several advantages: they are straight, and they do not shrink or warp. Also, they are easy to install, and are prepunched to provide for electrical lines and piping. One disadvantage of light-gauge steel studs, sometimes called "drywall studs," is that the gypsum drywall and trim must be attached with screws.

Standard dimensions are nearly identical to those of dimension lumber, with flange widths about 1-1/2 inches (38 mm) and web depths that range from a nominal 2 to 6 or more inches (51 to 72 mm). Gauges ranging from 22 to 26 are available, with partitions typically using the lighter gauge. A similar section of "track" is used in place of top and bottom plates as well as for "blocking," and is available prepunched. Light-gauge steel partition walls are usually constructed by installing top and bottom tracks and then snapping in the wall studs. It is not necessary to fasten the studs to the track.

More information on light-gauge steel partitions may be found in *Alternatives to Lumber and Plywood in Home Construction*,[1] prepared by the NAHB Research Center and published by HUD, or from the American Iron and Steel Institute.[2]

Framing Interior Door Openings

Openings in nonload-bearing partitions for passage doors, closets, etc., have no particular structural requirements. Standard interior passage doors do not add significant loads to the framing. Thus, the opening may be single-framed with one stud at each side and a block across the head. Cripples are not required over the head. With no structural loads on the partition, no header or jacks are required. Closet door openings may be framed similarly.

Walk-in closets are usually fitted with standard hinged passage doors. However, with typical 2-foot-deep (610 mm) closets that may be 4 to 8 feet (1.22 to 2.44 m) wide, bifold or sliding doors are often used to provide better access. An added benefit is that these doors do not require trim. If the closet width is planned to correspond with standard bifold or sliding closet door widths, no extra framing is required for a "stub" wall to form the required door opening width. If the closet width is greater than the door opening, a single stub wall should be used at one side or the other—rather than shorter stub walls on each side—to form the required opening with a minimum of framing. Framing may be further simplified by using ceiling height bifolds or sliders on closets, thus making it possible to eliminate all framing over the opening.

It should be noted that framing details often affect the cost of finish. Either inside or outside corners formed by framing at walls or ceilings add to the cost of finishing. A framing detail that

---

[1]*Alternatives to Lumber and Plywood in Home Construction.* NAHB Research Center. Prepared for the U.S. Department of Housing and Urban Development, Washington, DC. 1993.

[2]American Iron & Steel Institute, 1101 17th Street, NW, Suite 1300, Washington, DC.

minimizes corners around a closet opening will usually save on framing as well as on finishing costs.

The attic access opening should be carefully planned to avoid interrupting a truss or ceiling joist. Properly planned, an attic access opening in a closet, hallway, or other suitable location may be provided by simply installing two blocks between trusses or ceiling joists to form the opening.

Anchoring Partitions to the Structure

As discussed in Chapter 4, partitions may be nailed directly to a 5/8- or 3/4-inch (16 or 19 mm) subfloor regardless of their orientation. Parallel nonload-bearing partitions falling between floor framing members are adequately supported by the subfloor and do not require extra framing or blocking between floor joists. The bottom plate may be nailed directly to the subfloor without any special provisions.

Partitions that run perpendicular to the direction of the ceiling framing are simply nailed through the plates to the trusses or joists at each intersection. Partitions that run parallel to ceiling framing members may be fastened directly to these members when they are sufficiently close to permit nailing. However, because partitions are not necessarily positioned on the 2-foot (610 mm) module, they often fall somewhere between the ceiling framing members. When this occurs, the top of the partition may be supported with 2x3 or 2x4 blocks installed between overhead joists or trusses (see Figure 4.6). Blocks should be spaced 24 inches (610 mm) apart to provide backup for the ceiling finish as well.

As discussed in Chapter 5, a "partition post" is not required for attachment of partitions at the exterior wall. However, it is a good idea to use a mid-height block between exterior wall studs to secure the partition stud where it joins the wall. Of course, if the partition should be located sufficiently close to an exterior wall stud, it may be fastened directly to the stud and blocking would not be necessary.

Partition Intersections

Corners and other intersections of interior partitions are handled in much the same manner as that described for exterior walls. Corners may be formed by simply nailing the two end studs of the meeting walls together where they meet. "T"-intersections require only a mid-height block between studs to secure the end stud of the intersecting wall.

There are several alternative methods of providing the necessary backup for interior wall finish at partition intersections as described in Chapter 5. They consist of metal drywall "clips" spaced up to 2 feet (610 mm) apart or 1x3 lumber strips. The drywall is not fastened to the metal clips or wood backers. The sheet supported by the backers is installed first so that it will be held in place by the adjacent sheet when it is installed and nailed in place. This arrangement provides the recommended "floating joint" to help avoid cracking at the corner.

These same methods may be used to provide drywall backup at the ceiling. However, this is not often necessary. When partitions are perpendicular to ceiling framing, no additional backup is required. When parallel partitions fall between overhead members, the 24-inch (610 mm) on-center blocking discussed previously provides the necessary backup. In either case, nailing should be held back about 12 inches (305 mm) from the corner at the ceiling to provide a floating joint.

INTERIOR WALL AND CEILING FINISH

Gypsum wallboard, commonly known as "drywall," is universally used for interior wall and ceiling surfaces. It is a cost-effective, field-tolerant material that provides a uniform, stable surface for finishing. The most common gypsum drywall product is 1/2-inch-thick (13 mm) 4-foot-wide (1.22 m) sheets from 8 to 16 feet (2.44 to 4.87 m) in length, which is acceptable for use on stud spacings of 16 or 24 inches (406 or 610 mm). The long edges of panels are tapered to facilitate finishing with reinforcing tape and joint compound.

Typically, 4- x 12-foot (1.22 x 3.66 m) sheets are applied perpendicular to framing members on both walls and ceilings. Blocking is not required behind tapered edges. Ceiling panels are installed first, holding nails back about 12 inches (305 mm) wherever they abut a wall. Upper wall panels are then installed against the ceiling to support the edge of ceiling panels, holding nails back at least 6 inches (152 mm) from the wall-ceiling corner joint. This provides a "floating joint" to help avoid corner cracking (see Figure 7.1). No nails are used at the top wall plate.

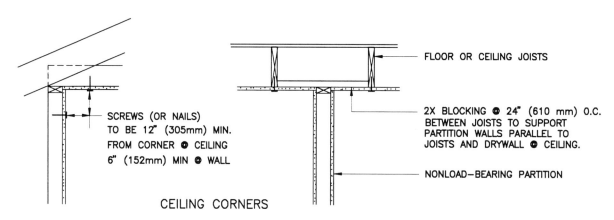

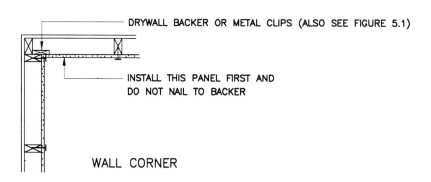

FIGURE 7.1 Floating Joint in Drywall Installation

With a 7-foot 7-inch (2.29 m) rough ceiling height, it is necessary to trim approximately 6 inches (152 mm) off the bottom edge of lower wall panels. This eliminates the tapered edge at that point and provides a flat surface to permit installation of base trim without shimming out the bottom edge. It is unnecessary to nail the drywall at the bottom wall plate where it is secured by base trim that is nailed through the drywall.

The National Gypsum Company recommends the use of either nails or screws for attaching gypsum wallboard to wood framing.[1] Nails should be GWB-54 located a minimum of 3/8-inch (10 mm) and a maximum of 1/2-inch (13 mm) from edges and ends of wallboard. Nails should be spaced a maximum of 7 inches (178 mm) on center for ceilings and 8 inches (203 mm) on center for walls. Where double nailing is used, the first nails are driven 12 inches (305 mm) on center for walls and ceilings and the second nails within 2 inches (51 mm) of the first; the first nail is struck again in the process to make certain the board is held tight to the framing.

Drywall screws are a highly effective means of attaching drywall to the wall framing and are finding an increase in use. Screw application can produce a higher-quality job at little or no additional cost while reducing the chances of "nail pops." Drywall screws should be 1-1/4-inch (32 mm) Type W spaced 12 inches (305 mm) on center for ceilings, and 16 inches (406 mm) on center for sidewalls with 16-inch (406 mm) stud spacing and 12 inches (305 mm) on center on sidewalls with 24-inch (610 mm) stud spacing.

Adhesive may also be used for attaching drywall, usually in conjunction with nails or screws. Installation recommendations vary with the wallboard product, the adhesive selected, and the type of framing used.

INTERIOR TRIM AND MILLWORK

Several basic molding shapes perform the primary function of covering most interior joints. Use of a paint finish on trim permits the use of lower-cost finger-joined wood trim or alternative materials (see section on Interior Decorating, p. 83).

The primary function of base molding is to cover the joint at the base of the wall. Wall-to-wall carpeting has eliminated the need for shoe molding since the carpet is normally installed directly against or under the base molding. In some cases, the base itself may be eliminated if drywall is fitted sufficiently close to the floor so that the joint is covered by carpeting. However, a base molding protects the wall finish from vacuum cleaners and furnishings, etc., and should not be omitted without considering local market preferences. A plastic cove molding supplied by the flooring installer is often used in lieu of a base molding for resilient floors. This avoids a return trip by the carpenter to install a shoe molding.

---

[1]Gypsum Wallboard Construction for Walls and Ceilings. National Gypsum Company, Gold Bond Building Products, Charlotte, NC. 1989.

The purpose of window trim is to cover the joints and corners created by the presence of a window opening. Window trim usually ends up being covered by curtains or drapes and may contribute little to the finished appearance of a home. A cost-effective option is to eliminate trim at the head and jambs and, instead, return the drywall into the window opening. A wood sill is then used to finish the opening with a small piece of trim to cover the joint beneath the sill. The joint where the drywall or sill meets the window should be sealed with caulk. Figure 7.2 presents an example of window trim details.

Interior Doors and Trim

Prehung interior doors can save a significant amount of on-site labor and contribute to accuracy at little or no extra cost. Prehung door units include door, jamb, and usually trim. Doors are hinged to the jamb and bored for the lockset. Both solid and split jambs are available. Solid jambs must fit the finished wall thickness and are installed by shimming and nailing. The casing is then installed on each side of the opening.

Split jambs have a tongue-and-groove or shiplap joint that permits the inside half of the jamb (with the door) to be separated from the outside half. Each half has the trim preinstalled. The inside half is installed first by nailing through the casing, then shimming and nailing at the hinges and latch plate. The outside half is then inserted and nailed through the casing. Although split jamb units cost slightly more than the solid type, they provide tolerance for variations in wall thickness and reduce construction time.

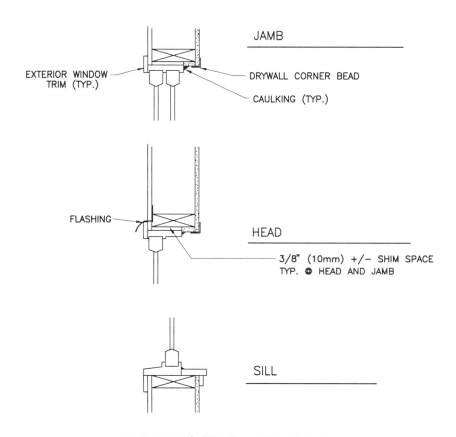

FIGURE 7.2 Window Trim Details

The most cost-effective interior passage door is a flush hollow-core hardboard door. This type of door is also available with a "wood grain" textured face or with a traditional six-panel "colonial" design at some extra cost. The hardboard takes a paint finish well and may be painted at the same time as the walls. An additional coat of semigloss paint is often applied for better durability and cleanability. Other variations come prefinished with simulated wood grains.

Closet Doors and Trim

As noted previously, standard interior passage doors are usually used for walk-in closets while 2-foot-deep (610 mm) wardrobe closets are often fitted with bifold or double sliding doors for better access. Sliding doors provide an inherent tolerance in opening width because they close satisfactorily even if the opening is slightly narrower than specified. However, this type of door limits access to one-half of the closet at a time.

Bifold doors, on the other hand, permit full access to the closet by opening both doors at the same time. A variety of styles, including steel, wood, or mirrored as well as ceiling-height models, are generally available. Steel bifold doors are especially stable and provide relatively trouble-free action. Installation is simple, with ample adjustments provided to compensate for minor inaccuracies in the opening size. No trim is required around closet openings with most types of bifold or sliding doors.

A variety of techniques and products are available for providing shelf and hanger storage in a closet. These include prefinished metal shelves with accompanying brackets, telescoping metal closet bars, and related specialty products. While these products may simplify installation, the added cost can be out of proportion to the benefit. The most cost-effective solution is often a simple 3/4- x 12-inch (19 x 305 mm) particleboard shelf with a rounded edge, and a standard closet pole. These can be painted along with the wall. However, particleboard should never be used to span more than 36 inches (914 mm) without intermediate support, or it will sag over time.

The simplest means of supporting shelf ends is with 1x4 lumber cleats nailed to the sidewalls. For nailing purposes, the cleats should be 2 feet (610 mm) long to span the distance between sidewall studs. A 45° bevel at the front edge of the cleat provides clearance for door operation and a more finished appearance. A 1x4 cleat is sufficiently wide to provide for attachment of a closet pole; a 1x2 cleat is adequate for supporting a shelf without a closet pole as in a linen closet. A "hook strip" across the back of the shelf is not required.

Intermediate support for longer shelves is easily provided with a metal bracket that also provides intermediate support for the closet pole. The bracket should be solidly attached through the drywall into a stud at the back of the closet.

Stairways

As discussed in Chapter 2, stairways should be oriented parallel to floor joists so that the fewest number of structural members are interrupted. Where possible, the stairwell should be coordinated with the location of a regularly occurring joist at one side or the other to minimize the number of members required to frame the opening.

The most cost-effective type of stairs is a 3-foot-wide (914 mm) straight run, "boxed" stair with walls on both sides. More complex stair designs with landings, winders, open sides, and other special conditions add to cost and installation time. The basic boxed stair construction consists of treads and risers built into a routed stringer at each side. The height of the risers is adjusted to the number of steps and total height (rise) required to reach the upper floor level. The fewest number of steps in keeping with the maximum allowable riser height will provide optimum cost effectiveness and minimize the total length (run) of the stairs and related floor space requirements.

The One- and Two-Family Dwelling Code limits riser height to a maximum of 8-1/4 inches (210 mm) and tread width to a minimum of 9 inches (229 mm), with a maximum nosing of 1-1/2 inches (38 mm).[1] Stairs with 12 risers at 8-1/4 inches (210 mm) have a total rise of 8 feet 3 inches (2.52 m), which corresponds to a 7-foot 7-inch (2.31 m) rough ceiling height with a 2x8 floor system at the top (see Figure 7.3). The stairs would then have 11 treads at 9 inches (229 mm) for a total run of 8 feet 3 inches (2.51 m).

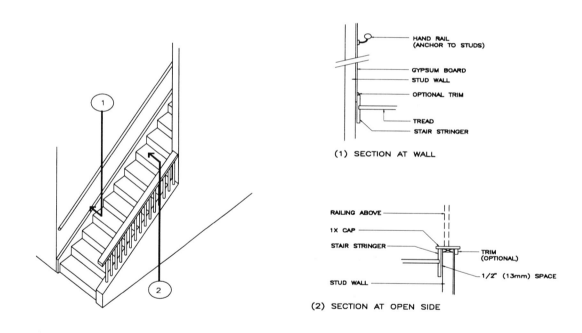

FIGURE 7.3 Stairway Construction

---

[1]CABO One- and Two-Family Dwelling Code, 1992 Edition, Section R-213.1. Council of American Building Officials, Falls Church, VA. 1992.

The minimum stairway width allowed is 3 feet (914 mm). A rough framing width of 3 feet, 1 inch (940 mm) allows a 1/2-inch (13 mm) space for drywall at each side. If stairs are installed before the drywall, the stringers should be nailed to wall studs at each side with a 1/2-inch-thick (13 mm) wood shim between the stringer and the stud. A small cove molding may be used to finish the joint after the drywall is in place. A prefinished handrail may then be mounted to the wall at one side after painting the stair trim to finish the stair installation.

It is sometimes desirable to open a portion of the stairway to an adjacent foyer, hall, or room to improve the appearance or to increase the lighting. Where desired, an open side may be created with a basic boxed stair at minimal cost without cutting away the stringer. Wall framing can be built flush with the top of the stringer in the open portion and trimmed with a 1x cap as shown in Figure 7.3. A prefinished guard rail may then be mounted on top of the cap after painting.

INTERIOR DECORATING

Today, latex paints (either flat or semigloss) are used almost universally for interior walls and, where painted, interior trim. New gypsum wallboard surfaces normally need no special preparation before painting. All surfaces should be dry, clean, and free of dust, dirt, oil, wax, and other contaminants.

A flat paint tends to conceal minor irregularities in walls and ceilings. An off-white paint enhances lighting, increases the apparent size of rooms, and blends with any decor. De-emphasizing trim by color matching to the walls helps create an uncluttered appearance—especially important in smaller rooms. Similarly, interior doors and stairs may be simplified and de-emphasized by painting with a matching color. Most trim may be installed before painting the interior and then painted together with walls and ceilings. Where practical, prefinished items such as paneling, cabinets, bifold closet doors, flooring, etc., should be installed after painting to minimize masking labor and paint damage. Painting contractors can easily spray paint an entire house interior in this way in a day. The use of multiple interior colors increases the cost and complicates interior decorating.

A semigloss paint is often used in kitchens and bathrooms to provide better serviceability. Similarly, a semigloss paint may be used on interior trim and doors. A semigloss color that matches the flat paint hides paint lines where the two types of paint meet. Textured paint is sometimes used on ceilings for appearance, and can help cover irregularities. However, this type of paint is applied separately and can cost two to three times as much as regular spray paint.

Where relief from painted walls is desired, decorative wall coverings may be used at some additional cost. Wallpaper is available in an endless variety of patterns and colors and may be used on a single accent wall or to cover all walls in a room. Decorative wall coverings are usually offered as options due to variations in taste. It is usually easier to market a new home without preselected wall coverings that the buyer may find unattractive.

Bathroom Walls

The walls immediately surrounding bathtubs and showers require a waterproof finish and should be covered with moisture-resistant drywall. Four and one/fourth-inch-square (108 mm) self-spacing tile is then applied directly to the moisture-resistant drywall with a waterproof adhesive made for this purpose. Tiles are generally installed to a height of about 6 feet (1.83 m). After allowing time for the adhesive to set, all joints are grouted except at the top of the tub or shower base and at corners. These joints should be filled with an elastic caulking compound such as silicone "tub caulk" to avoid subsequent cracking.

Traditionally, ceramic tile has been used to complete the finish. Fiberglass-reinforced plastic tub and shower units with an integral wall surround provide a jointless, leak-proof enclosure. Their use avoids additional treatment of tub and shower walls and can eliminate a separate trade from the construction process. Whether a fiberglass or ceramic tile wall surround is used, special care should be taken to caulk around the faucet and tub spout to prevent water from gaining access at these critical points. Leaking water can cause serious damage to the floor, walls, and ceiling below.

Medicine cabinets are normally required for storage of day-to-day toiletry items. The least costly installation is a surface mounted cabinet which is simply attached to the wall. Since this type of cabinet does not extend into the wall, it may be used with any wall construction, without interfering with plumbing or wiring that might be present in the wall.

Kitchen Cabinets

Kitchen cabinets and counter tops constitute a major cost item in a typical new home and should be carefully planned to be cost-effective. Prefabricated cabinets are generally less costly than custom-made cabinetry. However, in certain cases, custom cabinets can be less costly if properly planned. Further, a "pantry" can often be substituted for cabinet space at less cost.

It is wise to lay out the kitchen and to select cabinets based on available cabinet sizes. Pre-fabricated base and wall cabinets usually range in width from 12 to 36 inches (305 to 914 mm) in increments of 3 inches (76 mm). The standard height of base cabinets is 36 inches (914 mm), while heights of wall cabinets range from 12 to 30 inches (305 to 762 mm). With careful planning, cabinets may be reduced to a minimum number of standard sizes; wider cabinets cost less per linear foot. If several houses are designed with the same kitchen layout, a savings may be incurred through bulk ordering from the supplier.

Prefabricated cabinets are typically installed with 3-inch-long (76 mm) wood screws fastened through the drywall into wall studs. Base cabinets are set in place and anchored through the top rail at the rear. Wall cabinets are anchored to the wall through rails at the top and bottom. Wall cabinets do not need to be anchored into a bulkhead at the top.

A bulkhead is not required over kitchen cabinets. Standard wall cabinets may be hung at a 7-foot (2.13 m) height, leaving an open shelf across the top. Wall cabinets may also be extended to the ceiling. With a 7-foot 6-inch (2.29 m) ceiling height, a 6-inch (152 mm) extension is all that is required. This may be accomplished by increasing the overall height of the cabinets, which increases storage capacity, or by installing a 6-inch-high (152 mm) filler panel of matching wood at the top.

Counter tops are economical and are generally available from the same source as cabinets. Laminated plastic counter tops provide a serviceable and decorative surface. They are normally available in either a "post-formed" or "self-edged" construction. The post-formed type is desirable because it has fewer joints and a raised edge to catch spills. Minimizing the choice of colors simplifies ordering, stocking, and construction. Counter tops are custom fabricated with the hole precut for the kitchen sink. Care should be taken to ensure that accurate kitchen layout dimensions are given to the fabricator.

FINISH FLOORS

Finish floors may be grouped into three categories: wall-to-wall carpeting, resilient flooring, and specialty floors. Several varieties of each type of flooring are available to add the final touch to a home.

Wall-to-Wall Carpet

Wall-to-wall carpeting is widely used as the standard floor covering for bedrooms, living areas, halls, and stairways. Wall-to-wall carpet may be installed directly over concrete or single-layer wood floors. It is tolerant of minor imperfections in the underlying floor construction and provides a uniform, appealing floor covering. Together with a suitable pad, carpeting softens the impact of concrete floors and provides some thermal protection. Regardless of the subfloor construction, a heavier pad can be used to provide a more luxurious "feel" at little extra cost.

Whether the underlying floor is wood or concrete, carpeting is usually installed with "tack" strips of 1/4-inch (6 mm) plywood with upward-protruding barbs. The strips are installed around the room perimeter and the pad is installed within the strips. The carpet is then stretched over the tack strips and anchored by pressing down over the barbs. Wall-to-wall carpeting is generally installed right up to the base; no shoe molding is necessary. Little scrap or waste is necessary with careful measurement and fitting. Major areas are covered first. Trim pieces may then be used in closets and other small areas. Carpet may be installed directly to the floor in closets without using tack strips or a pad.

Wall-to-wall carpet is one of the last items installed in a new home after all construction trades have moved out. For this reason, if a house is sold before construction is complete, carpeting can be offered to home buyers in several choices of quality and color without disrupting the construction schedule.

Resilient Flooring

Resilient floorings are products that are installed as a thin veneer over the structural floor to provide a durable, easy-to-maintain surface. Resilient flooring is available in either tile or sheet form. Embossed patterns help mask any irregularities in the underlying floor—whether the floor construction is wood or concrete.

Vinyl sheet flooring is produced in a wide variety of colors, patterns, and qualities. The most popular vinyl sheet products consist of a clear vinyl wear surface bonded to a fibrous backing with a printed design in between. Some products also have a backing of vinyl foam to increase resiliency. Sheet floorings are usually installed with an adhesive. More recently, products have become available that may be installed with adhesive only at joints and around the perimeter.

The most widely used resilient tile product is a 12-inch-square (305 mm), 1/16-inch-thick (2 mm) vinyl tile. It is especially suitable over concrete floors, which provide a stable base, although it is also widely used over wood floor constructions. This product provides a serviceable, appealing floor at reasonable cost for kitchens, baths, family rooms, etc. Generally, there is less scrap and waste from installation of tile than with sheet flooring, as the tiles readily adapt to any room configuration.

Resilient flooring products may be applied directly to an underlayment grade, tongue-and-groove plywood subfloor, providing that it has been installed properly and protected from undue abuse during construction. Where the subfloor does not present an acceptable surface for one reason or another, particleboard, plywood, or hardboard underlayment should be used over the subfloor. The underlayment should be securely fastened to the subfloor with special nails or staples spaced at 3 inches (76 mm) along edges and 6 inches (152 mm) in both directions across the panel. The use of a construction adhesive provides additional assurance of secure attachment, especially at joints.

A small molding may be used to cover the joint around the edge of the finished flooring. A cost-effective alternative is to use plastic cove base in lieu of a wood base in rooms where resilient flooring is installed. This allows the flooring installer to complete the job without calling the carpenter back.

Specialty Floorings

Other types of products such as ceramic tile and hardwood floors are generally more costly. The home buyer may, however, prefer a special floor treatment in some rooms and may be willing to pay extra for it.

A common example of special floor treatment is ceramic tile for bathroom floors. Ceramic tile is available in fabric-backed sheets with tiles properly spaced and prearranged in patterns. The sheets may be applied directly to wood or concrete floor constructions with adhesive. After the adhesive has had time to set, the joints are filled with grout. Ceramic base is generally used with a ceramic tile floor.

Hardwood flooring has a strong appeal to many home buyers. Prefinished wood flooring allows installation in feature areas such as a family room without disrupting the construction schedule. Wood strip flooring is offered in various widths, but wider widths are more subject to warping and have a greater tendency to open up at joints with changes in moisture conditions. Tongue-and-groove strip flooring is generally blind-nailed to wood floor constructions by driving special nails down through the tongue at a 45° angle with a nailing machine designed for this purpose. Thinner variations of strip flooring are installed with adhesives. Some wood strip flooring may be applied over concrete floors using installation methods specified by the manufacturer, but caution is suggested.

Wood block or "parquet" flooring is also offered in a number of variations. One of the more common consists of a series of 5/16-inch-thick (8 mm) wood slats attached to each other to form a 7-inch (178 mm) square. These products are generally suitable for use over wood or concrete floor constructions. A special adhesive designed for this purpose is used for installation.

BIBLIOGRAPHY

American Concrete Institute (ACI). *Building Code Requirements for Reinforced Concrete (ACI 318-89) and Commentary*. Detroit, MI. 1990.

American Forest & Paper Association. *National Design Specification for Wood Construction*. Washington, DC. 1991.

____. *National Design Specification Supplement, Design Values for Wood Construction*. Washington, DC. 1991.

____. *Permanent Wood Foundation System: Design, Fabrication, and Installation Manual*. Washington, DC. 1987.

____. *Span Tables for Joists and Rafters*. Washington, DC. 1993.

American Institute of Timber Construction. *Timber Construction Manual, Third Edition*. John Wiley and Sons. New York, NY. 1985.

American Iron and Steel Institute. *Residential Steel Beam and Column Load/Span Tables*. Washington, DC. 1993.

American Plywood Association (APA). *APA Design/Construction Guide: Residential and Commercial*. Tacoma, WA. 1993.

____. *APA Product Guide: Grades and Specifications*. Tacoma, WA. 1988.

____. *APA Report T92-28: Roof Sheathing Fastening Schedules for Wind Uplift*. Tacoma, WA. 1993.

____. *Technical Note No. B-429: Non-Load Bearing Partitions on Plywood Floors*. Tacoma, WA.

American Society for Testing and Materials (ASTM). *Standard Practice for the Use of Metric (SI) Units in Building Design and Construction (Committee E-6 Supplement to E380) E621-84*. Philadelphia, PA. 1991.

____. *Standard Practice for the Use of the International System of Units (The Modernized Metric System) E 380-92*. Philadelphia, PA. 1992.

American Society of Civil Engineers (ASCE). *Minimum Design Loads for Buildings and Other Structures (ANSI/ASCE 7-88)*. New York, NY. 1990.

Building Officials and Code Administrators International, Inc. (BOCA). *The National Building Code*. Country Club Hills, IL. 1993.

Council of American Building Officials (CABO). *CABO One- and Two-Family Dwelling Code.* Falls Church, VA. 1992.

Fine Homebuilding: Foundations and Masonry. The Taunton Press. Newtown, CT. 1990.

Fine Homebuilding: Frame Carpentry. The Taunton Press. Newtown, CT. 1990.

Interagency Council on Metric Policy. The Construction Subcommittee of the Metrication Operating Committee. *Metric Guide for Federal Construction, First Edition.* Washington, DC. 1991.

National Association of Home Builders (NAHB). *Controlling Moisture in Homes.* Washington, DC. 1987.

NAHB Research Center. *Alternatives to Lumber and Plywood in Home Construction.* U.S. Department of Housing and Urban Development, Washington, DC. 1993.

____. *Frost- Protected Shallow Foundations in Residential Construction.* U.S. Department of Housing and Urban Development, Washington, DC. 1993.

____. *Insulation Manual—Homes/Apartments.* Upper Marlboro, MD. 1971.

____. *Manual of Lumber and Plywood-Saving Techniques for Residential Light-Frame Construction.* Upper Marlboro, MD. 1971.

____. *NAHB Research Report No. 4: Off-Center Spliced Floor Joists.* National Association of Home Builders, Washington, DC. 1982.

____. *NAHB Research Report No. 5: Plywood Headers for Residential Construction.* National Association of Home Builders, Washington, DC. 1983.

____. *Performance of Glued Single-Layer Plywood-to-Wood Joist Floor Systems.* U.S. Department of Housing and Urban Development, Washington, DC. 1973.

____. *Reducing Home Building Costs with Optimum Value Engineered Design and Construction.* U.S. Department of Housing and Urban Development, Washington, DC. 1977.

____. *Stemwall Foundations for Residential Construction.* U.S. Department of Housing and Urban Develoment, Washington, DC. 1993.

National Concrete Masonry Association. *Nonreinforced Concrete Masonry Design Tables.* Herndon, VA. 1971.

National Gypsum Company. Gold Bond Building Products. *Gypsum Wallboard Construction for Walls and Ceilings.* Charlotte, NC. 1989.

National Institute of Building Sciences. Construction Metrication Council. "Metric in Construction." *Construction Metrication Council Newsletter*. Washington, DC. January-February 1993.

National Research Council Canada. Associate Committee on the National Building Code. *Canadian Housing Code 1990*. Ottawa, ON, Canada. 1992.

Stalnaker, Judith J. and Ernest C. Harris. *Structural Design in Wood*. Van Nostrand Reinhold. New York, NY. 1989.

Truss Plate Institute. *HIB-91 Summary Sheet: Commentary and Recommendations for Handling, Installing, and Bracing Metal Plate Connected Wood Trusses*. Madison, WI. 1991.

U.S. Department of Agriculture Forest Service. Forest Products Laboratory. *Light-Frame Wall and Floor Systems, Analysis and Performance*. Washington, DC. 1989.

U.S. Department of Housing and Urban Development (HUD), Office of Policy Development and Research. Steven Winter Associates. *Home Building Cost Cuts: Construction Methods and Materials for Affordable Housing*. Washington, DC. 1981.

Wood Truss Council of America. *Wood Truss Handbook*. Madison, WI. 1993.

APPENDIX A
METRIC CONVERSIONS

TABLE A.1
Metric Conversion Factors

QUANTITY	From INCH-POUND UNITS	To METRIC UNITS	METRIC SYMBOL	MULTIPLY BY
Length	Mile	Kilometer	km	1.609344
	Foot	Meter	m	0.3048
	Inch	Millimeter	mm	25.4
Area	Square Foot	Square Meter	m²	0.09290304
	Square Inch	Square Millimeter	mm²	645.16
Mass	Pound	Kilogram	kg	0.453592
	Kip (1000 lb)	Metric Ton (1000 kg)	—	0.453592
Force	Pound	Newton	N	4.44822
Force/Unit Length	Pound per Lineal Foot (plf)	Newton per Meter	N/m	14.5939
Pressure	Pound Per Square Foot	Pascal	Pa	47.8803
	Pound Per Square Inch	Kilopascal	kPa	6.89476

Ref: *Metric Guide for Federal Construction*, First Edition. The Construction Subcommittee of the Metrication Operating Committee of the Interagency Council on Metric Policy, National Institute of Building Sciences, Washington, DC.

TABLE A.2
Hard Metric Conversions for Selected Building Materials

MATERIAL	INCH-POUND	HARD METRIC
Brick	varies	90 mm x 57 mm x 190 mm
Mortar Joints	⅜-inch or ½-inch	10 mm
Brick Module	2 feet x 2 feet	600 mm x 600 mm
Concrete Block	8 inch x 8 inch x 16 inch	190 mm x 190 mm x 390 mm
Stud Spacing[1]	16-inch	400 mm
	24-inch	600 mm
Drywall, Panels, and Rigid Insulation[2]	4 feet x 8 feet	1200 mm x 2400 mm
	4 feet x 10 feet	1200 mm x 3000 mm

Notes: [1]Cross-sections of timber members will stay the same.
[2]Thicknesses will stay the same so that fire, acoustic, and thermal ratings will not change.
Ref: *Metric in Construction*. Construction Metrication Council, National Institute of Building Sciences, Washington, DC. January-February 1993.

APPENDIX B
CONSTRUCTION SPECIFICATIONS

CUSTOMER _____ DATE _____

ADDRESS OR LOT NO. _____

HOUSE STYLE _____

EXTERIOR

Siding Type and Color _____   Gutter Color _____

Exterior Trim and Color _____   Overhead Door _____

Front Door Style and Color _____   Sliding Glass Door _____

Side Door Style and Color _____   Deadbolts _____

Roof Type and Color _____   Interior Hardware _____

Shutter Color _____   Exterior Hardware _____

Brick Veneer _____

INSULATION TYPE

Walls _____   R-Value _____

Floors _____   R-Value _____

Roof/Ceilings _____   R-Value _____

Basement Perimeter _____

FIREPLACE

Style _____   Mantel _____

Brick _____   Glass Doors _____

Hearth _____   Flue _____

WINDOWS

Location	Type	Manufacturer	Size	Sash-Material	Glass	Screens
Basement						
First Floor						
Second Floor						
Other						

MECHANICAL/ELECTRICAL

Electrical Service _____

Heat/AC Type and Size _____

INTERIOR PAINT

Foyer _____   D.R. _____   BR/2 _____   Main Bath _____

P.R. _____   P.R. _____   BR/3 _____   Master Bath _____

L.R. _____   MBR _____   BR/4 _____   Ceilings _____

Kitchen _____

INTERIOR TRIM

Door Style and Color _____

Trim Style, Stained or Painted _____

Handrail Style _____

OVERHEAD LIGHTING

Location	Style	Manufacturer
_____	_____	_____
_____	_____	_____
_____	_____	_____
_____	_____	_____

APPLIANCES

Range Model and Color _____   Disposal Model _____

Range Hood Model and Color _____   Dryer Fuel _____ Vented _____

Ducted or Non-Ducted _____   Hot Water Fuel _____ Size _____

Dishwasher Model and Color _____   Other _____

Refrigerator Model and Color _____

PLUMBING

	Number	Location	Type
Sink			
Lavatory			
Water closet			
Tub/Shower			
Shower			
Laundry			
Other			

BATHS

Main Bath	Master Bath	Powder Room
Walls _____	Walls _____	Towel Bars _____
Towel Bars _____	Towel Bars _____	Paper Holder _____
Shower Rod _____	Shower Rod _____	Other _____
Paper Holder _____	Paper Holder _____	
Other _____	Other _____	

FLOORS

Location	Type	Manufacturer
_____	_____	_____
_____	_____	_____
_____	_____	_____

CABINETS AND VANITIES

Kitchen Style _____	Powder Room Style _____	Main Bath Style _____	Master Bath Style _____
Supplor _____	Supplor _____	Supplor _____	Supplor _____
Hardware _____	Hardware _____	Hardware _____	Hardware _____
Top _____	Top _____	Top _____	Top _____

SIGNATURE _____   DATE _____

Ref.:   Adapted from *Housing Construction Process Flow Manual*. U.S. Department of Housing and Urban Development, Washington, DC. 1985.

APPENDIX C
DESIGN MAPS

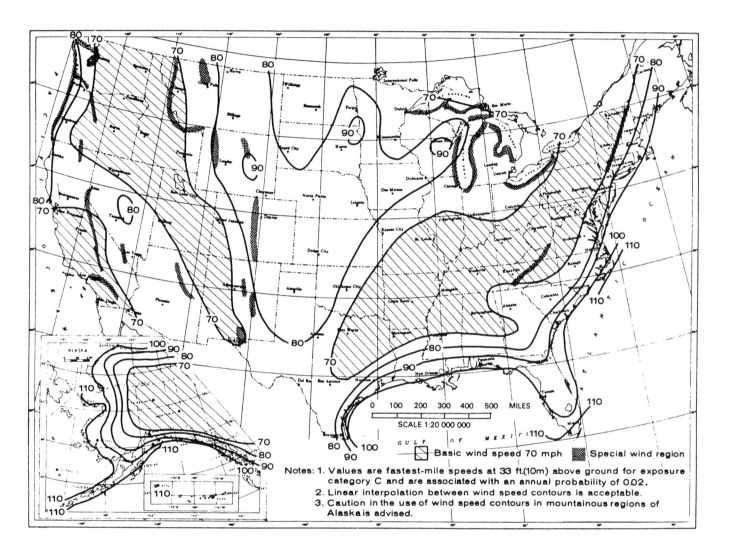

FIGURE C.1 Basic Wind Speed Map (mph)

1 mile = 1.609 kilometers

Ref: From *ASCE Standard 7-88, Minimum Design Loads for Buildings and Other Structures.* American
Society of Civil Engineers, New York, NY. 1990. Reproduced by permission of ASCE.

TABLE C.1
Design Wind Loads

EXPOSURE CLASSIFICATION	BASIC WIND SPEED (mph)		BUILDING HEIGHT										
			ONE STORY				TWO STORY				THREE STORY			
			WALLS		ROOF UPLIFT		WALLS		ROOF UPLIFT		WALLS		ROOF UPLIFT	
	mph	kph	psf	kPa	psf	kPa	psf	kPa	psf	kPa	psf	kPa	psf	kPa
A/B	80	129	N/A	N/A	N/A	N/A	N/A	N/A	N/A	N/A	N/A	N/A	N/A	N/A
	90	145	N/A	N/A	N/A	N/A	N/A	N/A	N/A	N/A	N/A	N/A	20	0.96
	100	161	N/A	N/A	N/A	N/A	N/A	N/A	21	1.01	N/A	N/A	25	1.20
C	70	113	N/A	N/A	N/A	N/A	N/A	N/A	N/A	N/A	N/A	N/A	N/A	N/A
	80	129	N/A	N/A	20	0.96	N/A	N/A	22	1.05	N/A	N/A	25	1.20
	90	145	N/A	N/A	26	1.24	N/A	N/A	28	1.34	N/A	N/A	31	1.48
	100	161	N/A	N/A	32	1.53	32	1.53	35	1.68	35	1.68	39	1.86
	110	177	35	1.68	38	1.82	38	1.82	42	2.01	43	2.06	47	2.25
D	70	113	N/A	N/A	20	0.96	N/A	N/A	22	1.05	N/A	N/A	24	1.15
	80	129	N/A	N/A	27	1.29	N/A	N/A	28	1.34	N/A	N/A	31	1.48
	90	145	32	1.53	37	1.77	36	1.72	40	1.92	39	1.86	43	2.06
	100	161	42	2.01	46	2.20	44	2.11	49	2.35	49	2.35	53	2.54
	110	177	50	2.39	55	2.63	54	2.59	59	2.82	59	2.82	64	3.06

Notes:

1. Select exposure classification from the descriptions below:
   Exposure A/B — Urban and suburban areas, wooded areas, or other terrain with numerous closely spaced obstructions having the size of single-family dwellings or larger in the upwind direction for a distance of at least 1,500 feet (457 m).
   Exposure C — Open terrain with scattered obstructions having heights generally less than 30 feet (9.1 m).
   Exposure D — Flat, unobstructed areas exposed to wind flowing over large bodies of water extending inland from the shoreline a distance of 1,500 feet (457 m).

2. Wind speeds may be obtained from Basic Wind Speed map. Wind speeds represent the following: 70 = 0 to 70 mph (113 = 0 to 113 kph); 80 = 71 to 80 mph (129 = 114 to 129 kph); 90 = 81 to 90 mph (145 = 130 to 145 mph); 100 = 91 to 100 mph (161 = 146 to 161 kph); 110 = 101 to 110 mph (177 = 162 to 177 kph). Hawaii has a basic wind speed of 80 mph (129 kph) and Puerto Rico has a basic wind speed of 95 mph (153 kph).

3. Building heights used to determine design wind loads are: one-story = 20 feet (6.1 m); two-story = 30 feet (9.1 m); and three-story = 50 feet (15.2 m). Interpolation between building height values and between map contours is acceptable.

4. Uplift loads act normal to the roof or overhang.

5. N/A = No design is required in accordance with Sections 402.3 and 702.10 of the One- and Two- Family Dwelling Code (CABO) for design wind loads on roofs less than 20 psf (0.96 kPa), and walls less than 30 psf (1.44 kPa).

6. Buildings over 50 feet (15.2 m) in height, or with unusual constructions or geometric shapes, with overhanging eave projections greater than 24 inches (610 mm), or located in special wind regions or localities shall be designed in accordance with the provisions of ASCE 7-88.

Ref: *CABO One- and Two-Family Dwelling Code*, 1992 Edition. Council of American Building Officials, Falls Church, Virginia. 1992.

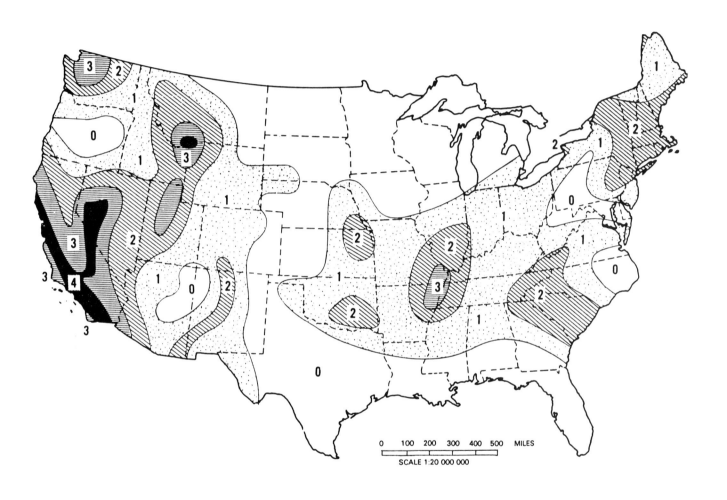

FIGURE C.2-a   Map for Seismic Zones—Contiguous 48 States
1 mile = 1.609 kilometers

Ref: From *ASCE Standard 7-88, Minimum Design Loads for Buildings and Other Structures,* American
Society of Civil Engineers, New York, NY. 1990. Reproduced by permission of ASCE.

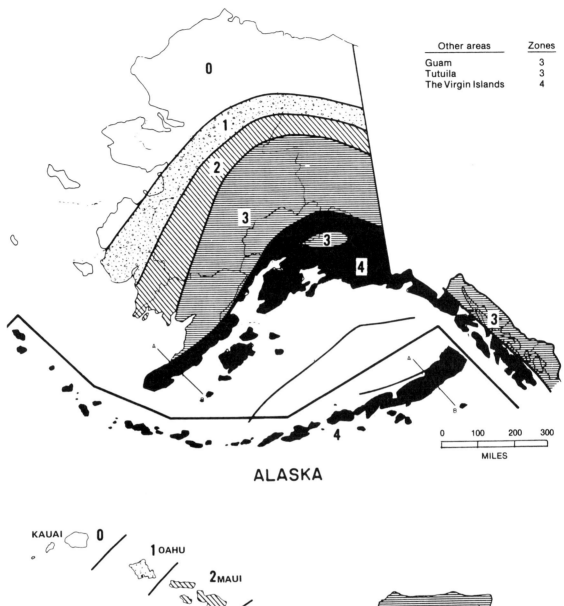

Other areas	Zones
Guam	3
Tutuila	3
The Virgin Islands	4

ALASKA

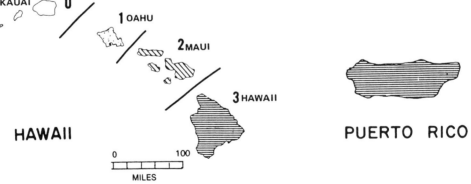

FIGURE C.2-b   Map for Seismic Zones—Hawaii, Alaska, and Puerto Rico
1 mile = 1.609 kilometers

Ref: From *ASCE Standard 7-88, Minimum Design Loads for Buildings and Other Structures*. American Society of Civil Engineers, New York, NY. 1990. Reproduced by permission of ASCE.

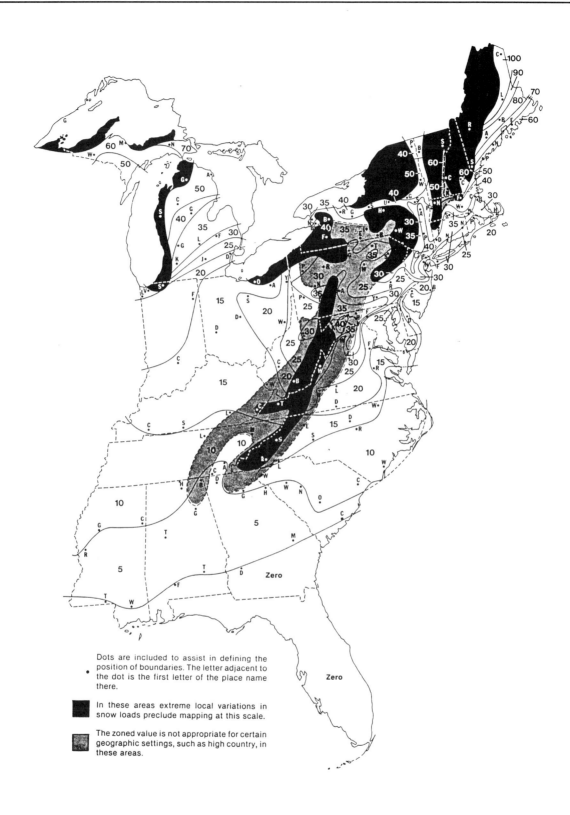

FIGURE C.3-a   Ground Snow Loads for the Eastern United States (psf)
1 psf = 47.9 Pa

Ref: Cold Regions Research and Engineering Laboratory, United States Corps of Engineers, Handover, NH.
1988. Used by Permission.

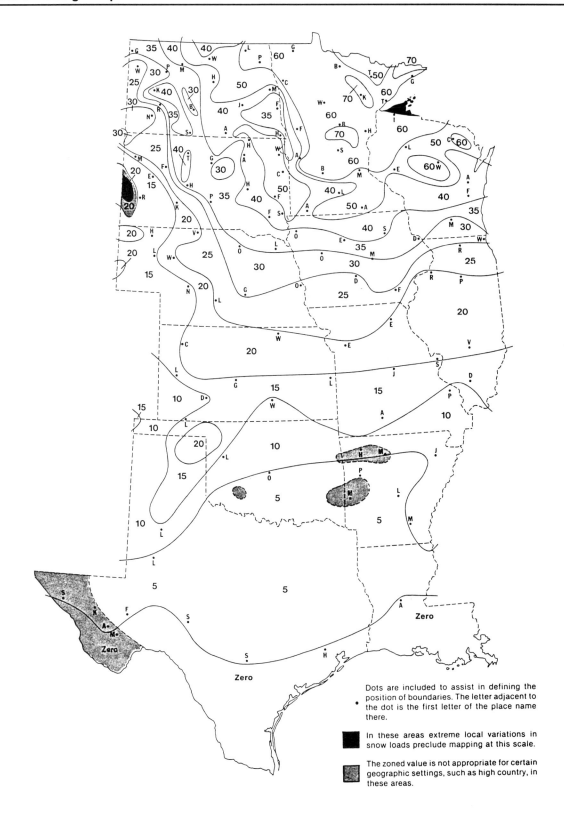

Dots are included to assist in defining the position of boundaries. The letter adjacent to the dot is the first letter of the place name there.

In these areas extreme local variations in snow loads preclude mapping at this scale.

The zoned value is not appropriate for certain geographic settings, such as high country, in these areas.

FIGURE C.3-b   Ground Snow Loads for the Central United States (psf)
1 psf = 47.9 Pa

Ref: Cold Regions Research and Engineering Laboratory, United States Corps of Engineers, Handover, NH. 1988. Used by Permission.

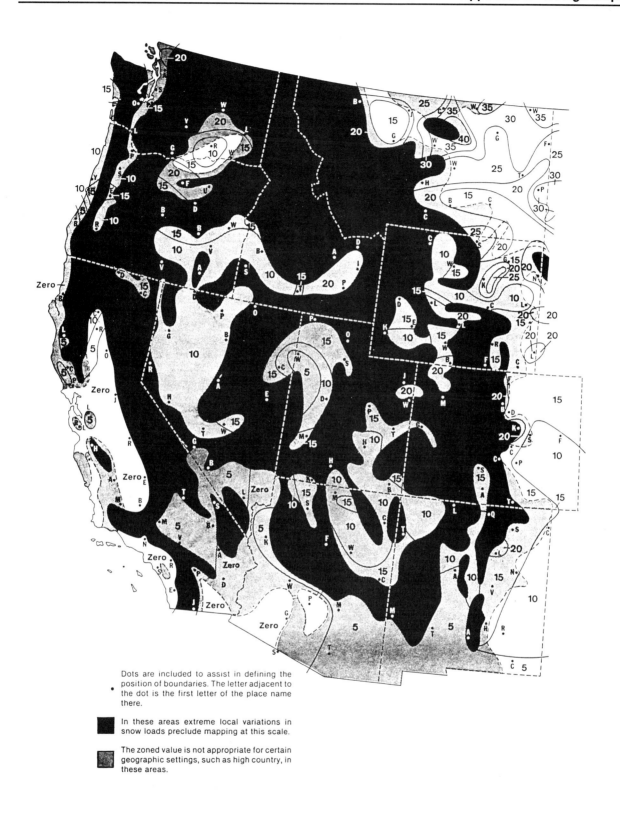

FIGURE C.3-c   Ground Snow Loads for the Western United States (psf)
1 psf = 47.9 Pa

Ref: Cold Regions Research and Engineering Laboratory, United States Corps of Engineers, Handover, NH. 1988. Used by Permission.

FIGURE C.4   Termite Infestation Probability Map

Ref: *CABO One- and Two-Family Dwelling Code*, 1992 Edition. Council of American Building Officials, Falls Church, VA. 1992.

FIGURE C.5   Decay Probability Map

Ref: *CABO One- and Two-Family Dwelling Code*, 1992 Edition. Council of American Building Officials, Falls Church, VA. 1992.

APPENDIX D
SECTION PROPERTIES

TABLE D.1
Section Properties of Standard Dressed (S4S) Sawn Lumber

NOMINAL SIZE b x d	STANDARD DRESSED SIZE (S4S) b x d inches x inches	AREA OF SECTION A in²	X-X AXIS		Y-Y AXIS		APPROXIMATE WEIGHT IN POUNDS PER LINEAR FOOT (lb/ft) OF PIECE WITH DENSITY OF WOOD EQUAL TO 40 lb/ft³
			SECTION MODULUS S_{xx} in³	MOMENT OF INERTIA I_{xx} in⁴	SECTION MODULUS S_{yy} in³	MOMENT OF INERTIA I_{yy} in⁴	
1 x 3	3/4 x 2-1/2	1.875	0.781	0.977	0.234	0.088	0.521
1 x 4	3/4 x 3-1/2	2.625	1.531	2.680	0.328	0.123	0.729
1 x 6	3/4 x 5-1/2	4.125	3.781	10.40	0.516	0.193	1.146
1 x 8	3/4 x 7-1/4	5.438	6.570	23.82	0.680	0.255	1.510
1 x 10	3/4 x 9-1/4	6.938	10.70	49.47	0.867	0.325	1.927
1 x 12	3/4 x 11-1/4	8.438	15.82	88.99	1.055	0.396	2.344
2 x 3	1-1/2 x 2-1/2	3.750	1.563	1.953	0.938	0.703	1.042
2 x 4	1-1/2 x 3-1/2	5.250	3.063	5.359	1.313	0.984	1.458
2 x 5	1-1/2 x 4-1/2	6.750	5.063	11.39	1.688	1.266	1.875
2 x 6	1-1/2 x 5-1/2	8.250	7.563	20.80	2.063	1.547	2.292
2 x 8	1-1/2 x 7-1/4	10.88	13.14	47.63	2.719	2.039	3.021
2 x 10	1-1/2 x 9-1/4	13.88	21.39	98.93	3.469	2.602	3.854
2 x 12	1-1/2 x 11-1/4	16.88	31.64	178.0	4.219	3.164	4.688
2 x 14	1-1/2 x 13-1/4	19.88	43.89	290.8	4.969	3.727	5.521
3 x 4	2-1/2 x 3-1/2	8.750	5.104	8.932	3.646	4.557	2.431
3 x 5	2-1/2 x 4-1/2	11.25	8.438	18.98	4.688	5.859	3.125
3 x 6	2-1/2 x 5-1/2	13.75	12.60	34.66	5.729	7.161	3.819
3 x 8	2-1/2 x 7-1/4	18.13	21.90	79.39	7.552	9.440	5.035
3 x 10	2-1/2 x 9-1/4	23.13	35.65	164.9	9.635	12.04	6.424
3 x 12	2-1/2 x 11-1/4	28.13	52.73	296.6	11.72	14.65	7.813
3 x 14	2-1/2 x 13-1/4	33.13	73.15	484.6	13.80	17.25	9.201
3 x 16	2-1/2 x 15-1/4	38.13	96.90	738.9	15.89	19.86	10.59
4 x 4	3-1/2 x 3-1/2	12.25	7.146	12.51	7.146	12.51	3.403
4 x 5	3-1/2 x 4-1/2	15.75	11.81	26.58	9.188	16.08	4.375
4 x 6	3-1/2 x 5-1/2	19.25	17.65	48.53	11.23	19.65	5.347
4 x 8	3-1/2 x 7-1/4	25.38	30.66	111.1	14.80	25.90	7.049
4 x 10	3-1/2 x 9-1/4	32.38	49.91	230.8	18.89	33.05	8.993
4 x 12	3-1/2 x 11-1/4	39.38	73.83	415.3	22.97	40.20	10.94
4 x 14	3-1/2 x 13-1/4	46.38	102.4	678.5	27.05	47.34	12.88
4 x 16	3-1/2 x 15-1/4	53.38	135.7	1034	31.14	54.49	14.83
5 x 5	4-1/2 x 4-1/2	20.25	15.19	34.17	15.19	34.17	5.625
6 x 6	5-1/2 x 5-1/2	30.25	27.73	76.26	27.73	76.26	8.403
6 x 8	5-1/2 x 7-1/2	41.25	51.56	193.4	37.81	104.0	11.46
6 x 10	5-1/2 x 9-1/2	52.25	82.73	393.0	47.90	131.7	14.51
6 x 12	5-1/2 x 11-1/2	63.25	121.2	697.1	57.98	159.4	17.57
6 x 14	5-1/2 x 13-1/2	74.25	167.1	1128	68.06	187.2	20.63
6 x 16	5-1/2 x 15-1/2	85.25	220.2	1707	78.15	214.9	23.68
6 x 18	5-1/2 x 17-1/2	96.25	280.7	2456	88.23	242.6	26.74
6 x 20	5-1/2 x 19-1/2	107.3	348.6	3398	98.31	270.4	29.79
6 x 22	5-1/2 x 21-1/2	118.3	423.7	4555	108.4	298.1	32.85
6 x 24	5-1/2 x 23-1/2	129.3	606.2	5948	118.5	325.8	35.90

| NOMINAL SIZE b x d | STANDARD DRESSED SIZE (S4S) b x d | AREA OF SECTION A | X-X AXIS | | Y-Y AXIS | | APPROXIMATE WEIGHT IN POUNDS PER LINEAR FOOT (lb/ft) OF PIECE WITH DENSITY OF WOOD EQUAL TO 40 lb/ft^3 |
| | | | SECTION MODULUS S_{xx} | MOMENT OF INERTIA I_{xx} | SECTION MODULUS S_{yy} | MOMENT OF INERTIA I_{yy} | |
	inches x inches	in^2	in^3	in^4	in^3	in^4	
8 x 8	7-1/2 x 7-1/2	56.25	70.31	263.7	70.31	263.7	15.63
8 x 10	7-1/2 x 9-1/2	71.25	112.8	535.9	89.06	334.0	19.79
8 x 12	7-1/2 x 11-1/2	86.25	165.3	950.5	107.8	404.3	23.96
8 x 14	7-1/2 x 13-1/2	101.3	227.8	1538	126.6	474.6	28.13
8 x 16	7-1/2 x 15-1/2	116.3	300.3	2327	145.3	544.9	32.29
8 x 18	7-1/2 x 17-1/2	131.3	382.8	3350	164.1	615.2	36.46
8 x 20	7-1/2 x 19-1/2	146.3	475.3	4634	182.8	685.5	40.63
8 x 22	7-1/2 x 21-1/2	161.1	577.8	6211	201.6	755.9	44.79
8 x 24	7-1/2 x 23-1/2	176.3	690.3	8111	220.3	826.2	48.96
10 x 10	9-1/2 x 9-1/2	90.25	142.9	678.8	142.9	678.8	25.07
10 x 12	9-1/2 x 11-1/2	109.3	209.4	1204	173.0	821.7	30.35
10 x 14	9-1/2 x 13-1/2	128.3	288.6	1948	203.1	964.5	35.63
10 x 16	9-1/2 x 15-1/2	147.3	380.4	2948	233.1	1107	40.90
10 x 18	9-1/2 x 17-1/2	166.3	484.9	4243	263.2	1250	46.18
10 x 20	9-1/2 x 19-1/2	185.3	602.1	5870	293.3	1393	51.46
10 x 22	9-1/2 x 21-1/2	204.3	731.9	7868	323.4	1536	56.74
10 x 24	9-1/2 x 23-1/2	223.3	874.4	10270	353.5	1679	62.01
12 x 12	11-1/2 x 11-1/2	132.3	253.5	1458	253.5	1458	36.74
12 x 14	11-1/2 x 13-1/2	155.3	349.3	2358	297.6	1711	43.13
12 x 16	11-1/2 x 15-1/2	178.3	460.5	3569	341.6	1964	49.51
12 x 18	11-1/2 x 17-1/2	201.3	587.0	5136	385.7	2218	55.90
12 x 20	11-1/2 x 19-1/2	224.3	728.8	7106	429.8	2471	62.29
12 x 22	11-1/2 x 21-1/2	247.3	886.0	9524	473.9	2725	68.68
12 x 24	11-1/2 x 23-1/2	270.3	1058	12440	518.0	2978	75.07
14 x 14	13-1/2 x 13-1/2	182.3	410.1	2768	410.1	2768	50.63
14 x 16	13-1/2 x 15-1/2	209.3	540.6	4189	470.8	3178	58.13
14 x 18	13-1/2 x 17-1/2	236.3	689.1	6029	531.6	3588	65.63
14 x 20	13-1/2 x 19-1/2	263.3	855.6	8342	592.3	3998	73.13
14 x 22	13-1/2 x 21-1/2	290.3	1040	11180	653.1	4408	80.63
14 x 24	13-1/2 x 23-1/2	317.3	1243	14600	713.8	4818	88.13
16 x 16	15-1/2 x 15-1/2	240.3	620.6	4810	620.6	4810	66.74
16 x 18	15-1/2 x 17-1/2	271.3	791.1	6923	700.7	5431	75.35
16 x 20	15-1/2 x 19-1/2	302.3	982.3	9578	780.8	6051	83.96
16 x 22	15-1/2 x 21-1/2	333.3	1194	12840	860.9	6672	92.57
16 x 24	15-1/2 x 23-1/2	364.3	1427	16760	941.0	7293	101.2
18 x 18	17-1/2 x 17-1/2	306.3	893.2	7816	893.2	7816	85.07
18 x 20	17-1/2 x 19-1/2	341.3	1109	10810	995.3	8709	94.79
18 x 22	17-1/2 x 21-1/2	376.3	1348	14490	1097	9602	104.5
18 x 24	17-1/2 x 23-1/2	411.3	1611	18930	1199	10500	114.2
20 x 20	19-1/2 x 19-1/2	380.3	1236	12050	1236	12050	105.6
20 x 22	19-1/2 x 21-1/2	419.3	1502	16150	1363	13280	116.5
20 x 24	19-1/2 x 23-1/2	458.3	1795	21090	1489	14520	127.3
22 x 22	21-1/2 x 21-1/2	462.3	1656	17810	1656	17810	128.4
22 x 24	21-1/2 x 23-1/2	505.3	1979	23250	1810	19460	140.3
24 x 24	23-1/2 x 23-1/2	552.3	2163	25420	2163	25420	153.4

Ref: *National Design Specification Supplement*, 1991 Edition. American Forest & Paper Association, Washington, DC. 1991. Used by permission of AFPA.

TABLE D.2
Section Properties of Standard Dressed (S4S) Sawn Lumber

NOMINAL SIZE	STANDARD DRESSED SIZE (S4S)		AREA OF SECTION	X-X AXIS		Y-Y AXIS		APPROXIMATE WEIGHT IN NEWTONS PER METER (N/m) OF PIECE WITH DENSITY OF WOOD EQUAL TO
	WIDTH	HEIGHT		SECTION MODULUS	MOMENT OF INERTIA	SECTION MODULUS	MOMENT OF INERTIA	
$b \times d$	b	d	A	S_{xx}	I_{xx}	S_{yy}	I_{yy}	
inches	mm	mm	m^2	m^3	m^4	m^3	m^4	641 kg/m³
1 x 3	19.05	63.50	0.1210	0.01280	0.004067	0.003835	0.0003663	7.603
1 x 4	19.05	88.90	0.1694	0.02509	0.01115	0.005375	0.0005120	10.64
1 x 6	19.05	139.7	0.2661	0.06196	0.04329	0.008456	0.0008033	16.73
1 x 8	19.05	184.2	0.3508	0.1077	0.09915	0.01114	0.001061	22.04
1 x 10	19.05	235.0	0.4476	0.1753	0.2059	0.01421	0.001353	28.12
1 x 12	19.05	285.8	0.5444	0.2592	0.3704	0.01729	0.001648	34.21
2 x 3	38.10	63.50	0.2419	0.02561	0.008129	0.01537	0.002926	15.21
2 x 4	38.10	88.90	0.3387	0.05019	0.02231	0.02152	0.004096	21.28
2 x 5	38.10	114.3	0.4355	0.08297	0.04741	0.02766	0.005269	27.36
2 x 6	38.10	139.7	0.5323	0.1239	0.08658	0.03381	0.006439	33.45
2 x 8	38.10	184.2	0.7019	0.2153	0.1982	0.04456	0.008487	44.09
2 x 10	38.10	235.0	0.8955	0.3505	0.4118	0.05685	0.01083	56.24
2 x 12	38.10	285.8	1.089	0.5185	0.7409	0.06914	0.01317	68.42
2 x 14	38.10	336.6	1.283	0.7192	1.210	0.08143	0.01551	80.57
3 x 4	63.50	88.90	0.5645	0.08364	0.03718	0.05975	0.01897	35.48
3 x 5	63.50	114.3	0.7258	0.1383	0.07900	0.07682	0.02439	45.61
3 x 6	63.50	139.7	0.8871	0.2065	0.1443	0.09388	0.02981	55.73
3 x 8	63.50	184.2	1.170	0.3589	0.3304	0.1238	0.03929	73.48
3 x 10	63.50	235.0	1.492	0.5842	0.6864	0.1579	0.05011	93.75
3 x 12	63.50	285.8	1.815	0.8641	1.234	0.1921	0.06098	114.0
3 x 14	63.50	336.6	2.137	1.199	2.017	0.2261	0.07180	134.3
3 x 16	63.50	387.4	2.460	1.588	3.076	0.2604	0.08266	154.5
4 x 4	88.90	88.90	0.7903	0.1171	0.05207	0.1171	0.05207	49.66
4 x 5	88.90	114.3	1.016	0.1935	0.1106	0.1506	0.06693	63.85
4 x 6	88.90	139.7	1.242	0.2892	0.2020	0.1840	0.08179	78.03
4 x 8	88.90	184.2	1.637	0.5024	0.4624	0.2425	0.1078	102.9
4 x 10	88.90	235.0	2.089	0.8179	0.9607	0.3096	0.1376	131.2
4 x 12	88.90	285.8	2.541	1.210	1.729	0.3764	0.1673	159.7
4 x 14	88.90	336.6	2.992	1.678	2.824	0.4433	0.1970	188.0
4 x 16	88.90	387.4	3.444	2.224	4.304	0.5103	0.2268	216.4
5 x 5	114.3	114.3	1.306	0.2489	0.1422	0.2489	0.1422	82.09
6 x 6	139.7	139.7	1.952	0.4544	0.3174	0.4544	0.3174	122.6
6 x 8	139.7	190.5	2.661	0.8449	0.8050	0.6196	0.4329	167.2
6 x 10	139.7	241.3	3.371	1.356	1.636	0.7849	0.5482	211.8
6 x 12	139.7	292.1	4.081	1.986	2.902	0.9501	0.6635	256.4
6 x 14	139.7	342.9	4.790	2.738	4.695	1.115	0.7792	301.1
6 x 16	139.7	393.7	5.500	3.608	7.105	1.281	0.8945	345.6
6 x 18	139.7	444.5	6.210	4.600	10.22	1.446	1.010	390.2
6 x 20	139.7	495.3	6.923	5.713	14.14	1.611	1.125	434.8
6 x 22	139.7	546.1	7.632	6.943	18.96	1.776	1.241	479.4
6 x 24	139.7	596.9	8.342	8.295	24.76	1.942	1.356	523.9

NOMINAL SIZE b x d	STANDARD DRESSED SIZE (S4S) WIDTH b	STANDARD DRESSED SIZE (S4S) HEIGHT d	AREA OF SECTION A	X-X AXIS SECTION MODULUS S_{xx}	X-X AXIS MOMENT OF INERTIA I_{xx}	Y-Y AXIS SECTION MODULUS S_{yy}	Y-Y AXIS MOMENT OF INERTIA I_{yy}	APPROXIMATE WEIGHT IN NEWTONS PER METER (N/m) OF PIECE WITH DENSITY OF WOOD EQUAL TO 641 kg/m³
inches	mm	mm	m²	m³	m⁴	m³	m⁴	
8 x 8	190.5	190.5	3.629	1.152	1.098	1.152	1.098	228.1
8 x 10	190.5	241.3	4.597	1.848	2.231	1.459	1.390	288.8
8 x 12	190.5	292.1	5.565	2.709	3.956	1.767	1.683	349.7
8 x 14	190.5	342.9	6.535	3.733	6.402	2.075	1.975	410.5
8 x 16	190.5	393.7	7.503	4.921	9.686	2.381	2.268	471.2
8 x 18	190.5	444.5	8.471	6.273	13.94	2.689	2.561	532.1
8 x 20	190.5	495.3	9.439	7.789	19.29	2.996	2.853	593.0
8 x 22	190.5	546.1	10.39	9.468	25.85	3.304	3.146	653.7
8 x 24	190.5	596.9	11.37	11.31	33.76	3.610	3.439	714.5
10 x 10	241.3	241.3	5.823	2.342	2.825	2.342	2.825	365.9
10 x 12	241.3	292.1	7.052	3.431	5.011	2.835	3.420	442.9
10 x 14	241.3	342.9	8.277	4.729	8.108	3.328	4.015	520.0
10 x 16	241.3	393.7	9.503	6.234	12.27	3.820	4.608	596.9
10 x 18	241.3	444.5	10.73	7.946	17.66	4.313	5.203	673.9
10 x 20	241.3	495.3	11.95	9.867	24.43	4.806	5.798	751.0
10 x 22	241.3	546.1	13.18	11.99	32.75	5.300	6.393	828.1
10 x 24	241.3	596.9	14.41	14.33	42.75	5.793	6.989	905.0
12 x 12	292.1	292.1	8.535	4.154	6.069	4.154	6.069	536.2
12 x 14	292.1	342.9	10.02	5.724	9.815	4.877	7.122	629.4
12 x 16	292.1	393.7	11.50	7.546	14.86	5.598	8.175	722.5
12 x 18	292.1	444.5	12.99	9.619	21.38	6.320	9.232	815.8
12 x 20	292.1	495.3	14.47	11.94	29.58	7.043	10.29	909.1
12 x 22	292.1	546.1	15.95	14.52	39.64	7.766	11.34	1002
12 x 24	292.1	596.9	17.44	17.34	51.78	8.488	12.40	1096
14 x 14	342.9	342.9	11.76	6.720	11.52	6.720	11.52	738.9
14 x 16	342.9	393.7	13.50	8.859	17.44	7.715	13.23	848.3
14 x 18	342.9	444.5	15.25	11.29	25.09	8.711	14.93	957.8
14 x 20	342.9	495.3	16.99	14.02	34.72	9.706	16.64	1067
14 x 22	342.9	546.1	18.73	17.04	46.53	10.70	18.35	1177
14 x 24	342.9	596.9	20.47	20.37	60.77	11.70	20.05	1286
16 x 16	393.7	393.7	15.50	10.17	20.02	10.17	20.02	974.0
16 x 18	393.7	444.5	17.50	12.96	28.82	11.48	22.61	1100
16 x 20	393.7	495.3	19.50	16.10	39.87	12.80	25.19	1225
16 x 22	393.7	546.1	21.50	19.57	53.44	14.11	27.77	1351
16 x 24	393.7	596.9	23.50	23.38	69.76	15.42	30.36	1477
18 x 18	444.5	444.5	19.76	14.64	32.53	14.64	32.53	1242
18 x 20	444.5	495.3	22.02	18.17	44.99	16.31	36.25	1383
18 x 22	444.5	546.1	24.28	22.09	60.31	17.98	39.97	1525
18 x 24	444.5	596.9	26.54	26.40	78.79	19.65	43.70	1667
20 x 20	495.3	495.3	24.54	20.25	50.16	20.25	50.16	1541
20 x 22	495.3	546.1	27.05	24.61	67.22	22.34	55.28	1700
20 x 24	495.3	596.9	29.57	29.41	87.78	24.40	60.44	1858
22 x 22	546.1	546.1	29.83	27.14	74.13	27.14	74.13	1874
22 x 24	546.1	596.9	32.60	32.43	96.77	29.66	81.00	2048
24 x 24	596.9	596.9	35.63	35.45	105.8	35.45	105.8	2239

Ref: Derived from the *National Design Specification Supplement*, 1991 Edition. American Forest & Paper Association, Washington, DC. 1991. Used by permission of AFPA.

APPENDIX E
BASE DESIGN VALUES

TABLE E.1
Base Design Values for Visually Graded Dimension Lumber, Selected Species
Use with Table E.1 and E.2 Adjustment Factors

SPECIES	COMMERCIAL GRADE	SIZE CLASSIFICA- TION	DESIGN VALUES IN POUNDS PER SQUARE INCH (psi)					
			BENDING F_b	TENSION PARALLEL TO GRAIN F_t	SHEAR PARALLEL TO GRAIN F_v	COMPRES- SION PERPEN- DICULAR TO GRAIN $F_{c\perp}$	COMPRES- SION PARALLEL TO GRAIN F_c	MODULUS OF ELASTICITY E
Douglas Fir-Larch	Select Structural		1,450	1,000	95	625	1,700	1,900,000
	No. 1 & Better	2"-4" thick	1,150	775	95	625	1,500	1,800,000
	No. 1		1,000	675	95	625	1,450	1,700,000
	No. 2	2" & wider	875	575	95	625	1,300	1,600,000
	No. 3		500	325	95	625	750	1,400,000
	Stud		675	450	95	625	825	1,400,000
	Construction	2"-4" thick	1,000	650	95	625	1,600	1,500,000
	Standard		550	375	95	625	1,350	1,400,000
	Utility	2"-4" wide	275	175	95	625	875	1,300,000
Douglas Fir-Larch (North)	Select Structural	2"-4" thick	1,300	800	95	625	1,900	1,900,000
	No. 1/No. 2		825	500	95	625	1,350	1,600,000
	No. 3	2" & wider	475	300	95	625	775	1,400,000
	Stud		650	375	95	625	850	1,400,000
	Construction	2"-4" thick	950	575	95	625	1,750	1,500,000
	Standard		525	325	95	625	1,400	1,400,000
	Utility	2"-4" wide	250	150	95	625	925	1,300,000
Hem-Fir	Select Structural		1,400	900	75	405	1,500	1,600,000
	No. 1 & Better	2"-4" thick	1,050	700	75	405	1,350	1,500,000
	No. 1		950	600	75	405	1,300	1,500,000
	No. 2	2" & wider	850	500	75	405	1,250	1,300,000
	No. 3		500	300	75	405	725	1,200,000
	Stud		675	400	75	405	800	1,200,000
	Construction	2"-4" thick	975	575	75	405	1,500	1,300,000
	Standard		550	325	75	405	1,300	1,200,000
	Utility	2"-4" wide	250	150	75	405	850	1,100,000
Hem-Fir (North)	Select Structural	2"-4" thick	1,300	775	75	370	1,650	1,700,000
	No. 1/No. 2		1,000	550	75	370	1,450	1,600,000
	No. 3	2" & wider	575	325	75	370	850	1,400,000
	Stud		775	425	75	370	925	1,400,000
	Construction	2"-4" thick	1,150	625	75	370	1,750	1,500,000
	Standard		625	350	75	370	1,500	1,400,000
	Utility	2"-4" wide	300	175	75	370	975	1,300,000
Spruce-Pine- Fir	Select Structural	2"-4" thick	1,250	675	70	425	1,400	1,500,000
	No. 1/No. 2		875	425	70	425	1,100	1,400,000
	No. 3	2" & wider	500	250	70	425	625	1,200,000
	Stud		675	325	70	425	675	1,200,000
	Construction	2"-4" thick	975	475	70	425	1,350	1,300,000
	Standard		550	275	70	425	1,100	1,200,000
	Utility	2"-4" wide	250	125	70	425	725	1,100,000

Note: Tabulated design values are for normal load duration and dry service conditions. See the National Design Specification 2.3 for a comprehensive description of design value adjustment factors.

See Appendix F for Southern Pine Species. For other species such as, Aspen, Beech, Birch, Hickory, Cottonwood, Douglas Fir-south, Eastern Hemlock, Tamarack, Eastern Softwoods, Eastern White Pine, Mixed Maple, Mixed Oak, Northern Red Oak, Northern Species, Northern White Cedar, Red Maple, Red Oak, Redwood, Spruce-Pine-Fir-south, Western Cedars, Western Woods, White Oak and Yellow Poplar, consult the manufacturer or the National Design Specification for the Base Design Values.

Lumber Dimensions. Tabulated design values are applicable to lumber that will be used under dry conditions such as in most covered structures. For 2" to 4" thick lumber the DRY dressed sizes shall be used (see NDS® Table 1A) regardless of the moisture content at the time of manufacture or use. In calculation design values, the natural gain in strength and stiffness that occurs as lumber dries has been taken into consideration as well as the reduction in size that occurs when unseasoned lumber shrinks. The gain in load carrying capacity due to increased strength and stiffness resulting from drying more than offsets the design effect of size reductions due to shrinkage.

Stress-Rated Boards. Stress-rated boards of nominal 1", 1¼" and 1½" thickness, 2" and wider, of most species, are permitted the design values shown for Select Structural, No. 1 & Btr, No. 1, No. 2, No. 3, Stud, Construction, Standard, Utility, Clear Heart Structural and Clear Structural grades as shown in the 2" to 4" thick categories herein, when graded in accordance with the stress-rated board provisions in the applicable grading rules. Information on stress-rated board grades applicable to the various species is available from the respective grading rules agencies. Information on additional design values may also be available from the respective grading agencies.

Ref: *National Design Specification Supplement*, 1991 Edition. American Forest & Paper Association, Washington, DC. 1991. Used by permission of AFPA.

TABLE E.2
Base Design Values for Visually Graded Dimension Lumber, Selected Species
Use with Table E.1 and E.2 Adjustment Factors

SPECIES	COMMERCIAL GRADE	SIZE CLASSIFICATION	DESIGN VALUES IN KILOPASCALS (kPa)					
			BENDING F_b	TENSION PARALLEL TO GRAIN F_t	SHEAR PARALLEL TO GRAIN F_v	COMPRESSION PERPENDICULAR TO GRAIN $F_{c\perp}$	COMPRESSION PARALLEL TO GRAIN F_c	MODULUS OF ELASTICITY E
Doulas Fir-Larch	Select Structural		9,997	6,895	655	4,309	11,721	13,100,044
	No. 1 & Better	51-102 mm thick	7,929	5,343	655	4,309	10,342	12,410,568
	No. 1		6,895	4,654	655	4,309	9,997	11,721,092
	No. 2	51 mm & wider	6,033	3,964	655	4,309	8,963	11,031,616
	No. 3		3,447	2,241	655	4,309	5,171	9,652,664
	Stud		4,654	3,103	655	4,309	5,688	9,652,664
	Construction	51-102 mm thick	6,895	4,482	655	4,309	11,032	10,342,140
	Standard		3,792	2,586	655	4,309	9,308	9,652,664
	Utility	51-102 mm wide	1,896	1,207	655	4,309	6,033	8,963,188
Douglas Fir-Larch (North)	Select Structural	51-102 mm thick	8,963	5,516	655	4,309	13,100	13,100,044
	No. 1/No. 2		5,688	3,447	655	4,309	9,308	11,031,616
	No. 3	51 mm & wider	3,275	2,068	655	4,309	5,343	9,652,664
	Stud		4,482	2,586	655	4,309	5,861	9,652,664
	Construction	51-102 mm thick	6,550	3,964	655	4,309	12,066	10,342,140
	Standard		3,620	2,241	655	4,309	9,653	9,652,664
	Utility	51-102 mm wide	1,724	1,034	655	4,309	6,378	8,963,188
Hem-Fir	Select Structural		9,653	6,205	517	2,792	10,342	11,031,616
	No. 1 & Better	51-102 mm thick	7,239	4,826	517	2,792	9,308	10,342,140
	No. 1		6,550	4,137	517	2,792	8,963	10,342,140
	No. 2	51 mm & wider	5,861	3,447	517	2,792	8,618	8,963,188
	No. 3		3,447	2,068	517	2,792	4,999	8,273,712
	Stud		4,654	2,758	517	2,792	5,516	8,273,712
	Construction	51-102 mm thick	6,722	3,964	517	2,792	10,342	8,963,188
	Standard		3,792	2,241	517	2,792	8,963	8,273,712
	Utility	51-102 mm wide	1,724	1,034	517	2,792	5,861	7,584,236
Hem-Fir (North)	Select Structural	2"-4" thick	8,963	5,343	517	2,551	11,376	11,721,092
	No. 1/No. 2		6,895	3,792	517	2,551	9,997	11,031,616
	No. 3	51 mm & wider	3,964	2,241	517	2,551	5,861	9,652,664
	Stud		5,343	2,930	517	2,551	6,378	9,652,664
	Construction	51-102 mm thick	7,929	4,309	517	2,551	12,066	10,342,140
	Standard		4,309	2,413	517	2,551	10,342	9,652,664
	Utility	51-102 mm wide	2,068	1,207	517	2,551	6,722	8,963,188
Spruce-Pine-Fir	Select Structural	51-102 mm thick	8,618	4,654	483	2,930	9,653	10,342,140
	No. 1/No. 2		6,033	2,930	483	2,930	7,584	9,652,664
	No. 3	51 mm & wider	3,447	1,724	483	2,930	4,309	8,273,712
	Stud		4,654	2,241	483	2,930	4,654	8,273,712
	Construction	51-102 mm thick	6,722	3,275	483	2,930	9,308	8,963,188
	Standard		3,792	1,896	483	2,930	7,584	8,273,712
	Utility	51-102 mm wide	1,724	862	483	2,930	4,999	7,584,236

Note: Tabulated design values are for normal load duration and dry service conditions. See the National Design Specification 2.3 for a comprehensive description of design value adjustment factors.

See Appendix F for Southern Pine Species. For other species such as, Aspen, Beech, Birch, Hickory, Cottonwood, Douglas Fir- south, Eastern Hemlock, Tamarack, Eastern Softwoods, Eastern White Pine, Mixed Maple, Mixed Oak, Northern Red Oak, Northern Species, Northern White Cedar, Red Maple, Red Oak, Redwood, Spruce-Pine-Fir-south, Western Cedars, Western Woods, White Oak and Yellow Poplar, consult the manufacturer or the National Design Specification for the Base Design Values.

Lumber Dimensions. Tabulated design values are applicable to lumber that will be used under dry conditions such as in most covered structures. For 51 to 102 mm thick lumber the DRY dressed sizes shall be used (see NDS® Table 1A) regardless of the moisture content at the time of manufacture or use. In calculation design values, the natural gain in strength and stiffness that occurs as lumber dries has been taken into consideration as well as the reduction in size that occurs when unseasoned lumber shrinks. The gain in load carrying capacity due to increased strength and stiffness resulting from drying more than offsets the design effect of size reductions due to shrinkage.

Stress-Rated Boards. Stress-rated boards of nominal 25, 32, and 38 mm thickness, 51 mm and wider, of most species, are permitted the design values shown for Select Structural, No. 1 & Btr, No. 1, No. 2, No. 3, Stud, Construction, Standard, Utility, Clear Heart Structural and Clear Structural grades as shown in the 51 to 102 mm thick categories herein, when graded in accordance with the stress-rated board provisions in the applicable grading rules. Information on stress-rated board grades applicable to the various species is available from the respective grading rules agencies. Information on additional design values may also be available from the respective grading agencies.

Ref: Derived from the National Design Specification Supplement, 1991 Edition. American Forest & Paper Association, Washington, DC. 1991. Used by permission of AFPA.

ADJUSTMENT FACTORS FOR TABLES E.1 AND E.2

The following adjustment factors are taken from the *National Design Specification for Wood Construction Supplement*. The National Design Specification should be consulted for the proper usage of the adjustment factors and additional adjustment factors that may apply.

Size Factor, C_F

Tabulated bending, tension, and compression parallel to grain design values for dimension lumber 2" to 4" (51 to 102 mm) thick shall be multiplied by the following size factors:

Size Factors, C_F

Grades	Width		F_b		F_t	F_c
			Thickness			
	inches	millimeters	2" & 3" (51 & 76 mm)	4" (102 mm)		
Select Structural, No. 1 and Btr. No. 1, No. 2, No. 3	2, 3 & 4	51, 76, & 102	1.5	1.5	1.5	1.15
	5	127	1.4	1.4	1.4	1.1
	6	152	1.3	1.3	1.3	1.1
	8	203	1.2	1.3	1.2	1.05
	10	254	1.1	1.2	1.1	1.0
	12	305	1.0	1.1	1.0	1.0
	14 and wider	356 and wider	0.9	1.0	0.9	0.9
Stud	2, 3 & 4	51, 76, & 102	1.1	1.1	1.1	1.05
	5 & 6	127 & 152	1.0	1.0	1.0	1.0
Construction and Standard	2, 3 & 4	51, 76, & 102	1.0	1.0	1.0	1.0
Utility	4	102	1.0	1.0	1.0	1.0
	2 & 3	51 & 76	0.4	---	0.4	0.6

Repetitive Member Factor, C_r

Bending design values, F_b, for dimension lumber 2" to 4" (51 to 102 mm) thick shall be multiplied by the repetitive member factor, $C_r = 1.15$, when such members are used as joists, truss chords, rafters, studs, planks, decking or similar members which are in contact or spaced not more than 24" (610 mm) on centers, are not less than 3 in number and are joined by floor, roof or other load distributing elements adequate to support the design load.

Wet Service Factor, C_M

When dimension lumber is used where moisture content will exceed 19 percent for an extended time period, design values shall be multiplied by the appropriate wet service factors from the following table:

Wet Service Factors, C_M

F_b	F_t	F_v	$F_{c\perp}$	F_c	E
0.85*	1.0	0.97	0.67	0.8**	0.9
*when $(F_b)(C_F) \leq 1150$ psi (7929 kPa), $C_M = 1.0$ **when $(F_c)(C_F) \leq 750$ psi (5171 kPa), $C_M = 1.0$					

Ref: *National Design Specification Supplement*, 1991 Edition. American Forest & Paper Association, Washington, DC. 1991. Used by permission of AFPA.

APPENDIX F
BASE DESIGN VALUES, SOUTHERN PINE

TABLE F.1
Base Design Values for Visually Graded Southern Pine Dimension Lumber
Use with Tables F.1 and F.2 Adjustment Factors

SPECIES	COMMERCIAL GRADE	SIZE CLASSIFICA-TION	DESIGN VALUES IN POUNDS PER SQUARE INCH (psi)					
			BENDING	TENSION PARALLEL TO GRAIN	SHEAR PARALLEL TO GRAIN	COMPRES-SION PERPEN-DICULAR TO GRAIN	COMPRES-SION PARALLEL TO GRAIN	MODULUS OF ELASTICITY
			F_b	F_t	F_v	$F_{c\perp}$	F_c	E
Southern Pine	Dense Select–	Structural	3,050	1,650	100	660	2,250	1,900,000
	Select Structural		2,850	1,600	100	565	2,100	1,800,000
	Non-Dense Sel.-	Structural	2,650	1,350	100	480	1,950	1,700,000
	No. 1 Dense		2,000	1,100	100	660	2,000	1,800,000
	No. 1	2"-4" thick	1,850	1,050	100	565	1,850	1,700,000
	No. 1 Non-	Dense	1,700	900	100	480	1,700	1,600,000
	No. 2 Dense	2"-4" wide	1,700	875	90	660	1,850	1,700,000
	No. 2		1,500	825	90	565	1,650	1,600,000
	No. 2 Non-	Dense	1,350	775	90	480	1,600	1,400,000
	No. 3		850	475	90	565	975	1,400,000
	Stud		875	500	90	565	975	1,400,000
	Construction	2"-4" thick	1,100	625	100	565	1,800	1,500,000
	Standard		625	350	90	565	1,500	1,300,000
	Utility	4" wide	300	175	90	565	975	1,300,000
	Dense Select -	Structural	2,700	1,500	90	660	2,150	1,900,000
	Select Structural		2,550	1,400	90	565	2,000	1,800,000
	Non-Dense Sel.-	Structural	2,350	1,200	90	480	1,850	1,700,000
	No. 1 Dense		1,750	950	90	660	1,900	1,800,000
	No. 1	2"-4" thick	1,650	900	90	565	1,750	1,700,000
	No. 1 Non-	Dense	1,500	800	90	480	1,600	1,600,000
	No. 2 Dense	5"-6" wide	1,450	775	90	660	1,750	1,700,000
	No. 2		1,250	725	90	565	1,600	1,600,000
	No. 2 Non-	Dense	1,150	675	90	480	1,500	1,400,000
	No. 3		750	425	90	565	925	1,400,000
	Stud		775	425	90	565	925	1,400,000
	Dense Select	Structural	2,450	1,350	90	660	2,050	1,900,000
	Select Structural		2,300	1,300	90	565	1,900	1,800,000
	Non-Dense Sel.-	Structural	2,100	1,100	90	480	1,750	1,700,000
	No. 1 Dense	2"-4" thick	1,650	875	90	660	1,800	1,800,000
	No. 1		1,500	825	90	565	1,650	1,700,000
	No. 1 Non-Den.	8" wide	1,350	725	90	480	1,550	1,600,000
	No. 2 Dense		1,400	675	90	660	1,700	1,700,000
	No. 2		1,200	650	90	565	1,550	1,600,000
	No. 2 Non-	Dense	1,100	600	90	480	1,450	1,400,000
	No. 3		700	400	90	565	875	1,400,000
	Dense Select	Structural	2,150	1,200	90	660	2,000	1,900,000
	Select Structural		2,050	1,100	90	565	1,850	1,800,000
	Non-Dense Sel.-	Structural	1,850	950	90	480	1,750	1,800,000
	No. 1 Dense	2"-4" thick	1,450	775	90	660	1,750	1,800,000
	No. 1		1,300	725	90	565	1,600	1,700,000
	No. 1 Non-Den.	10" wide	1,200	650	90	480	1,500	1,600,000
	No. 2 Dense		1,200	625	90	660	1,650	1,700,000
	No. 2		1,050	575	90	565	1,500	1,600,000
	No. 2 Non-Den.		950	550	90	480	1,400	1,400,000
	No. 3		600	325	90	565	850	1,400,000

SPECIES	COMMERCIAL GRADE	SIZE CLASSIFICA- TION	DESIGN VALUES IN POUNDS PER SQUARE INCH (psi)					
			BENDING F_b	TENSION PARALLEL TO GRAIN F_t	SHEAR PARALLEL TO GRAIN F_v	COMPRES- SION PERPEN- DICULAR TO GRAIN $F_{c\perp}$	COMPRES- SION PARALLEL TO GRAIN F_c	MODULUS OF ELASTICITY E
	Dense Select	Structural	2,050	1,100	90	660	1,950	1,900,000
	Select Structural		1,900	1,050	90	565	1,800	1,800,000
	Non-Dense Sel.-	Structural	1,750	900	90	480	1,700	1,700,000
	No. 1 Dense	2"-4" thick	1,350	725	90	660	1,700	1,800,000
	No. 1		1,250	675	90	565	1,600	1,700,000
	No. 1 Non-Den.	12" wide	1,150	600	90	480	1,500	1,600,000
	No. 2 Dense		1,150	575	90	660	1,600	1,700,000
	No. 2		975	550	90	565	1,450	1,600,000
	No. 2 Non-Den.		900	525	90	480	1,350	1,400,000
	No. 3		575	325	90	565	825	1,400,000

Notes: Tabulated design values are for normal load duration and dry service conditions, unless specified otherwise. See NDS® 2.3 for a comprehensive description of design value adjustment factors.

Lumber Dimensions. Tabulated design values are applicable to lumber that will be used under dry conditions such as in most covered structures. For 2 to 4 inches thick lumber the DRY dressed sizes shall be used (see Table 1A in NDS®) regardless of the moisture content at the time of manufacture or use. In calculating design values, the natural gain in strength and stiffness that occurs as lumber dries has been taken into consideration as well as the reduction in size that occurs when unseasoned lumber shrinks. The gain in load carrying capacity due to increased strength and stiffness resulting from drying more than offsets the design effect of size reductions due to shrinkage.

Stress-Rated Boards. Information for various grades of Southern Pine stress-rated boards of nominal 1", 1¼" and 1½" thickness, 2" and wider, is available from the Southern Pine Inspection Bureau (SPIB) in the "Standard Grading Rules for Southern Pine Lumber."

Spruce Pine. To obtain recommended design values for Spruce Pine graded to SPIB rules, multiply the appropriate design values for Mixed Southern Pine by the corresponding conversion factor shown below and round to the nearest 100,000 psi for E; to the next lower multiple of 5 psi for F_v and $F_{c\perp}$; to the next lower multiple of 50 psi for F_b, F_t and F_c if 1000 psi or greater, 25 psi otherwise.

For Mixed Southern Pine, and wet and dry service condition Design Values see the manufacturers tables or the National Design Specification.

Conversion Factors for Determining Design Values for Spruce Pine

	BENDING F_b	TENSION PARALLEL TO GRAIN F_T	SHEAR PARALLEL TO GRAIN F_v	COMPRESSION PERPENDICULAR TO GRAIN $F_{c\perp}$	COMPRESSION PARALLEL TO GRAIN F_c	MODULUS OF ELASTICITY E
Conversion Factor	0.784	0.784	0.965	0.682	0.766	0.807

Ref: *National Design Specification Supplement*, 1991 Edition. American Forest & Paper Association, Washington, DC. 1991. Used by permission of AFPA.

TABLE F.2
Base Design Values for Visually Graded Southern Pine Dimension Lumber
Use with Tables F.1 and F.2 Adjustment Factors

SPECIES	COMMERCIAL GRADE	SIZE CLASSIFICA-TION	DESIGN VALUES IN KILOPASCALS(kPa)					
			BENDING	TENSION PARALLEL TO GRAIN	SHEAR PARALLEL TO GRAIN	COMPRES-SION PERPEN-DICULAR TO GRAIN	COMPRES-SION PARALLEL TO GRAIN	MODULUS OF ELASTICITY
			F_b	F_t	F_v	$F_{c\perp}$	F_c	E
Southern Pine	Dense Select–	Structural	21,029	11,376	689	4,551	15,513	13,100,044
	Select Structural		19,650	11,032	689	3,896	14,479	12,410,568
	Non-Dense Sel.-	Structural	18,271	9,308	689	3,309	13,445	11,721,092
	No. 1 Dense		13,790	7,584	689	4,551	13,790	12,410,568
	No. 1	51-102 mm thick	12,755	7,239	689	3,896	12,755	11,721,092
	No. 1 Non-Den.		11,721	6,205	689	3,309	11,721	11,031,616
	No. 2 Dense	51-102 mm wide	11,721	6,033	621	4,551	12,755	11,721,092
	No. 2		10,342	5,688	621	3,896	11,376	11,031,616
	No. 2 Non-Den.		9,308	5,343	621	3,309	11,032	9,652,664
	No. 3		5,861	3,275	621	3,896	6,722	9,652,664
	Stud		6,033	3,447	621	3,896	6,722	9,652,664
	Construction	51-102 mm thick	7,584	4,309	689	3,896	12,411	10,342,140
	Standard		4,309	2,413	621	3,896	10,342	8,963,188
	Utility	102 mm wide	2,068	1,207	621	3,896	6,722	8,963,188
	Dense Select	Structural	18,616	10,342	621	4,551	14,824	13,100,044
	Select Structural		17,582	9,653	621	3,896	13,790	12,410,568
	Non-Dense Sel.	Structural	16,203	8,274	621	3,309	12,755	11,721,092
	No. 1 Dense		12,066	6,550	621	4,551	13,100	12,410,568
	No. 1	51-102 mm thick	11,376	6,205	621	3,896	12,066	11,721,092
	No. 1 Non-Den.		10,342	5,516	621	3,309	11,032	11,031,616
	No. 2 Dense	127-152mm wide	9,997	5,343	621	4,551	12,066	11,721,092
	No. 2		8,618	4,999	621	3,896	11,032	11,031,616
	No. 2 Non-Den.		7,929	4,654	621	3,309	10,342	9,652,664
	No. 3		5,171	2,930	621	3,896	6,378	9,652,664
	Stud		5,343	2,930	621	3,896	6,378	9,652,664
	Dense Select	Structural	16,892	9,308	621	4,551	14,134	13,100,044
	Select Structural		15,858	8,963	621	3,896	13,100	12,410,568
	Non-Dense Sel.	Structural	14,479	7,584	621	3,309	12,066	11,721,092
	No. 1 Dense	51-102 mm thick	11,376	6,033	621	4,551	12,411	12,410,568
	No. 1		10,342	5,688	621	3,896	11,376	11,721,092
	No. 1 Non-Den.	203 mm wide	9,308	4,999	621	3,309	10,687	11,031,616
	No. 2 Dense		9,653	4,654	621	4,551	11,721	11,721,092
	No. 2		8,274	4,482	621	3,896	10,687	11,031,616
	No. 2 Non-Den.		7,584	4,137	621	3,309	9,997	9,652,664
	No. 3		4,826	2,758	621	3,896	6,033	9,652,664
	Dense Select	Structural	14,824	8,274	621	4,551	13,790	13,100,044
	Select Structural		14,134	7,584	621	3,896	12,755	12,410,568
	Non-Dense Sel.	Structural	12,755	6,550	621	3,309	12,066	11,721,092
	No. 1 Dense	51-102 mm thick	9,997	5,343	621	4,551	12,066	12,410,568
	No. 1		8,963	4,999	621	3,896	11,032	11,721,092
	No. 1 Non-Den.	254 mm wide	8,274	4,482	621	3,309	10,342	11,031,616
	No. 2 Dense		8,274	4,309	621	4,551	11,376	11,721,092
	No. 2		7,239	3,964	621	3,896	10,342	11,031,616
	No. 2 Non-Den.		6,550	3,792	621	3,309	9,653	9,652,664
	No. 3		4,137	2,241	621	3,896	5,861	9,652,664
	Dense Select	Structural	14,134	7,584	621	4,551	13,445	13,100,044
	Select Structural		13,100	7,239	621	3,896	12,411	12,410,568
	Non-Dense Sel.	Structural	12,066	6,205	621	3,309	11,721	11,721,092
	No. 1 Dense	51-102 mm thick	9,308	4,999	621	4,551	11,721	12,410,568
	No. 1		8,618	4,654	621	3,896	11,032	11,721,092
	No. 1 Non-Den.	305 mm wide	7,929	4,137	621	3,309	10,342	11,031,616
	No. 2 Dense		7,929	3,964	621	4,551	11,032	11,721,092
	No. 2		6,722	3,792	621	3,896	9,997	11,031,616
	No. 2 Non-Den.		6,205	3,620	621	3,309	9,308	9,652,664
	No. 3		3,964	2,241	621	3,896	5,688	9,652,664

Notes: Tabulated design values are for normal load duration and dry service conditions, unless specified otherwise. See NDS® 2.3 for a comprehensive description of design value adjustment factors.

Lumber Dimensions. Tabulated design values are applicable to lumber that will be used under dry conditions such as in most covered structures. For 51 to 102 mm thick lumber the DRY dressed sizes shall be used (see Table 1A in NDS®) regardless of the moisture content at the time of manufacture or use. In calculating design values, the natural gain in strength and stiffness that occurs as lumber dries has been taken into consideration as well as the reduction in size that occurs when unseasoned lumber shrinks. The gain in load carrying capacity due to increased strength and stiffness resulting from drying more than offsets the design effect of size reductions due to shrinkage.

Stress-Rated Boards. Information for various grades of Southern Pine stress-rated boards of nominal 25 mm, 32 mm and 38 mm thickness, 51 mm and wider, is available from the Southern Pine Inspection Bureau (SPIB) in the "Standard Grading Rules for Southern Pine Lumber."

Spruce Pine. To obtain recommended design values for Spruce Pine graded to SPIB rules, multiply the appropriate design values for Mixed Southern Pine by the corresponding conversion factor shown below and round to the nearest 6,894,760 kPa for E; to the next lower multiple of 34 kPa for F_v and $F_{c\perp}$; to the next lower multiple of 345 kPa for F_b, F_t and F_c if 6895 kPa or greater, 172 kPa otherwise.

For Mixed Southern Pine, and wet and dry service condition Design Values see the manufacturers tables or the National Design Specification.

Conversion Factors for Determining Design Values for Spruce Pine

	BENDING F_b	TENSION PARALLEL TO GRAIN F_T	SHEAR PARALLEL TO GRAIN F_v	COMPRESSION PERPENDICULAR TO GRAIN $F_{c\perp}$	COMPRESSION PARALLEL TO GRAIN F_c	MODULUS OF ELASTICITY E
Conversion Factor	0.784	0.784	0.965	0.682	0.766	0.807

Ref: Derived from the *National Design Specification Supplement*, 1991 Edition. American Forest & Paper Association, Washington, DC. 1991. Used by permission of AFPA.

ADJUSTMENT FACTORS FOR TABLES F.1 AND F.2

The following adjustment factors are taken from the *National Design Specification for Wood Construction Supplement*. The National Design Specification should be consulted for the proper use of the adjustment factors and additional adjustment factors that may apply.

Size Factor, C_F

Appropriate size adjustment factors have already been incorporated in the tabulated design values for most thicknesses of Southern Pine and Mixed Southern Pine dimension lumber. For dimension lumber 4 inches (102 mm) thick, 8 inches (203 mm) and wider (all grades except Dense Structural 86, Dense Structural 72 and Dense Structural 65), tabulated bending design values, F_b, shall be permitted to be multiplied by the size factor, $C_F=1.1$. For dimension lumber wider than 12 inches (305 mm) (all grades except Dense Structural 86, Dense Structural 72 and Dense Structural 65), tabulated bending, tension and compression parallel to grain design values for 12 inches (305 mm) wide lumber shall be multiplied by the size factor, $C_F=0.9$. When the depth, d, of Dense Structural 86, Dense Structural 72 or Dense Structural 65 dimension lumber exceeds 12 inches (305 mm), the tabulated bending design value, F_b, shall be multiplied by the following size factor:

$$C_F = (12/d)^{1/9}, \qquad \text{where d is expressed in inches, or}$$

$$C_F = (305/d)^{1/9}, \qquad \text{where d is expressed in millimeters.}$$

Repetitive Member Factor, C_r

Bending design values, F_b, for dimension lumber 2 to 4 inches (51-102 mm) thick shall be multiplied by the repetitive member factor, $C_r = 1.15$, when such members are used as joists, truss chords, rafters, studs, planks, decking or similar members which are in contact or spaced not more than 24 inches (610 mm) on centers, are not less than 3 in number and are jointed by floor, roof or other load distributing elements adequate to support the design load.

Wet Service Factor, C_M

When dimension lumber is used where moisture content will exceed 19 percent for an extended time period, design values shall be multiplied by the appropriate wet service factors from the following table (for dense Structural 86, Dense Structural 72 and dense Structural 65 use tabulated design values for wet service conditions without further adjustment):

Wet Service Factors, C_M

F_b	F_t	F_v	$F_{c\perp}$	F_c	E
0.85*	1.0	0.97	0.67	0.8**	0.9
*when $(F_b)(C_F) \leq 1150$ psi (7929 kPa), $C_M = 1.0$					
**when $(F_c)(C_F) \leq 750$ psi (5171 kPa), $C_M = 1.0$					

Ref: Derived from the *National Design Specification Supplement*, 1991 Edition. American Forest & Paper Association, Washington, DC. 1991. Used by permission of AFPA.

APPENDIX G
REPRESENTATIVE ROOF TRUSS SPANS

TABLE G.1-a
Representative Roof Truss Spans for Selected Fink Trusses
for 24-inch on-center spacing with a total design load of 40 psf
and a load duration increase of 15 percent (feet-inches)

			TOP CHORD		BOTTOM CHORD	
			2x4	2x6	2x4	2x6
Southern Pine	3/12	#1 Dense	29-9	42-0[3]	31-11[3]	42-0[3]
		#1	28-11	42-0[3]	30-8[3]	40-9[3]
		#2 Dense	28-7	42-0[3]	28-8	40-7[3]
		#2	27-6	40-6	27-1	38-4
	4/12	#1 Dense	31-11[3]	42-0[3]	31-11[3]	42-0[3]
		#1	31-11[3]	42-0[3]	30-8[3]	40-9[3]
		#2 Dense	31-8	42-0[3]	29-10[3]	40-7[3]
		#2	30-7	42-0[3]	27-10[3]	39-1[3]
	5/12	#1 Dense	31-11[3]	42-0[3]	31-11[3]	42-0[3]
		#1	31-11[3]	42-0[3]	30-8[3]	40-9[3]
		#2 Dense	31-11[3]	42-0[3]	29-10[3]	40-7[3]
		#2	31-10	42-0[3]	27-10[3]	39-1[3]
Douglas Fir-Larch	3/12	Sel. Str.	30-5	43-2[3]	33-2[3]	43-2[3]
		#1 & Better	28-10	42-9	30-6[3]	41-9[3]
		#1	27-10	41-3	28-3[3]	40-3[3]
		#2	26-8	39-5	25-7[3]	37-9
	4/12	Sel. Str.	33-2[3]	43-2[3]	33-2[3]	43-2[3]
		#1 & Better	32-0	43-2[3]	30-6[3]	41-9[3]
		#1	30-11	43-2[3]	28-3[3]	40-3[3]
		#2	29-7	43-2[3]	25-7[3]	38-8[3]
	5/12	Sel. Str.	33-2[3]	43-2[3]	33-2[3]	43-2[3]
		#1 & Better	33-2[3]	43-2[3]	30-6[3]	41-9[3]
		#1	32-3	43-2[3]	28-3[3]	40-3[3]
		#2	30-10	43-2[3]	25-7[3]	38-8[3]
Spruce-Pine-Fir	3/12	Sel. Str.	28-2	38-5[3]	29-4[3]	28-5[3]
		#1	25-9	38-0	23-4	32-7
		#2	25-9	38-0	23-4	32-7
	4/12	Sel. Str.	29-4[3]	38-5[3]	29-4[3]	38-5[3]
		#1	28-9	38-5[3]	25-0[3]	36-5[3]
		#2	28-9	38-5[3]	25-0[3]	36-5[3]
	5/12	Sel. Str.	29-4[3]	38-5[3]	29-4[3]	38-5[3]
		#1	29-4[3]	38-5[3]	25-0[3]	36-5[3]
		#2	29-4[3]	38-5[3]	25-0[3]	36-5[3]
Hem-Fir	3/12	Sel. Str.	29-1	39-9[3]	30-9[3]	39-9[3]
		#1	26-10	39-7	26-10[3]	37-11[3]
		#2	25-8	37-9	24-5[3]	35-2[3]
	4/12	Sel. Str.	30-9[3]	39-9[3]	30-9[3]	39-9[3]
		#1	29-10	39-9[3]	26-10[3]	37-11[3]
		#2	28-6	39-9[3]	24-5[3]	35-2[3]
	5/12	Sel. Str.	30-9[3]	39-9[3]	30-9[3]	39-9[3]
		#1	30-9[3]	39-9[3]	26-10[3]	37-11[3]
		#2	29-8	39-9[3]	24-5[3]	35-2[3]

see notes at end of Table G.4-b

TABLE G.1-b
Representative Roof Truss Spans for Selected Fink Trusses
for 610 mm on-center spacing with a total design load of 1915 pa
and a load duration increase of 15 percent (meters)

			TOP CHORD		BOTTOM CHORD	
			2x4	2x6	2x4	2x6
Southern Pine	3/12	#1 Dense	9.07	12.80[3]	9.73[3]	12.80[3]
		#1	8.81	12.80[3]	9.35[3]	12.42[3]
		#2 Dense	8.71	12.80[3]	8.74	12.37[3]
		#2	8.38	12.34	8.25	11.68
	4/12	#1 Dense	9.73[3]	12.80[3]	9.73[3]	12.80[3]
		#1	9.73[3]	12.80[3]	9.35[3]	12.42[3]
		#2 Dense	9.65	12.80[3]	9.09[3]	12.37[3]
		#2	9.32	12.80[3]	8.48[3]	11.91[3]
	5/12	#1 Dense	9.73[3]	12.80[3]	9.73[3]	12.80[3]
		#1	9.73[3]	12.80[3]	9.35[3]	12.42[3]
		#2 Dense	9.73[3]	12.80[3]	9.09[3]	12.37[3]
		#2	9.70	12.80[3]	8.48[3]	11.91[3]
Douglas Fir-Larch	3/12	Sel. Str.	9.27	13.16[3]	10.11[3]	13.16[3]
		#1 & Better	8.79	13.03	9.30[3]	12.73[3]
		#1	8.48	12.57	8.61[3]	12.27[3]
		#2	8.13	12.01	7.80[3]	11.51
	4/12	Sel. Str.	10.11[3]	13.16[3]	10.11[3]	13.16[3]
		#1 & Better	9.75	13.16[3]	9.30[3]	12.73[3]
		#1	9.42	13.16[3]	8.61[3]	12.27[3]
		#2	9.02	13.16[3]	7.80[3]	11.79[3]
	5/12	Sel. Str.	10.11[3]	13.16[3]	10.11[3]	13.16[3]
		#1 & Better	10.11[3]	13.16[3]	9.30[3]	12.73[3]
		#1	9.83	13.16[3]	8.61[3]	12.27[3]
		#2	9.40	13.16[3]	7.80[3]	11.79[3]
Spruce-Pine-Fir	3/12	Sel. Str.	8.59	11.71[3]	8.94[3]	11.71[3]
		#1	7.85	11.58	7.11	9.93
		#2	7.85	11.58	7.11	9.93
	4/12	Sel. Str.	8.94[3]	11.71[3]	8.94[3]	11.71[3]
		#1	8.76	11.71[3]	7.62[3]	11.10[3]
		#2	8.76	11.71[3]	7.62[3]	11.10[3]
	5/12	Sel. Str.	8.94[3]	11.71[3]	8.94[3]	11.71[3]
		#1	8.94[3]	11.71[3]	7.62[3]	11.10[3]
		#2	8.94[3]	11.71[3]	7.62[3]	11.10[3]
Hem-Fir	3/12	Sel. Str.	8.86	12.12[3]	9.37[3]	12.12[3]
		#1	8.18	12.06	8.18[3]	11.56[3]
		#2	7.82	11.51	7.44[3]	10.72[3]
	4/12	Sel. Str.	9.37[3]	12.12[3]	9.37[3]	12.12[3]
		#1	9.09	12.12[3]	8.18[3]	11.56[3]
		#2	8.69	12.12[3]	7.44[3]	10.72[3]
	5/12	Sel. Str.	9.37[3]	12.12[3]	9.37[3]	12.12[3]
		#1	9.37[3]	12.12[3]	8.18[3]	11.56[3]
		#2	9.04	12.12[3]	7.44[3]	10.72[3]

see notes at end of Table G.4-b

TABLE G.2-a
Representative Roof Truss Spans for Selected Howe Trusses
for 24-inch on-center spacing with a total design load of 40 psf
and a load duration increase of 15 percent (feet-inches)

Species	Slope	Grade	TOP CHORD 2x4	TOP CHORD 2x6	BOTTOM CHORD 2x4	BOTTOM CHORD 2x6
Southern Pine	3/12	#1 Dense	29-6	43-9	37-10	43-9[2]
		#1	28-9	42-9	36-3	43-9[2]
		#2 Dense	28-4	41-11	32-3	43-9[2]
		#2	27-4	40-3	30-5	42-10
	4/12	#1 Dense	32-10	48-7	42-5	48-7[2]
		#1	32-0	47-5	40-9[3]	48-7[2]
		#2 Dense	31-6	46-5	37-3	48-7[2]
		#2	30-4	44-7	35-1	48-7[2]
	5/12	#1 Dense	34-3	50-7	42-5[3]	50-7[2]
		#1	33-4	49-5	40-9[3]	50-7[2]
		#2 Dense	32-10	48-4	39-8[3]	50-7[2]
		#2	31-8	46-4	36-11[3]	50-7[2]
Douglas Fir-Larch	3/12	Sel. Str.	30-2	44-9	44-0[3]	44-9[2]
		#1 & Better	28-7	42-6	37-3	44-9[2]
		#1	27-8	40-11	33-8	44-9[2]
		#2	26-6	39-2	30-5	42-8
	4/12	Sel. Str.	33-7	49-8	44-0[3]	49-8[2]
		#1 & Better	31-10	47-1	40-6[3]	49-8[2]
		#1	30-8	45-1	37-5[3]	49-8[2]
		#2	29-5	43-5	33-10[3]	48-11
	5/12	Sel. Str.	35-1	51-9	44-0[3]	51-9[2]
		#1 & Better	33-2	49-1	40-6[3]	51-9[2]
		#1	32-0	47-2	37-5[3]	51-9[2]
		#2	30-8	45-1	33-10[3]	51-4[3]
Spruce-Pine-Fir	3/12	Sel. Str.	27-11	41-4	35-6	41-4[2]
		#1	25-7	37-9	25-9	35-6
		#2	25-7	37-9	25-9	35-6
	4/12	Sel. Str.	31-1	45-11	38-11[3]	45-11[2]
		#1	28-6	42-0	30-2	42-0
		#2	28-6	42-0	30-2	42-0
	5/12	Sel. Str.	32-6	47-11	38-11[3]	47-11[2]
		#1	29-10	43-9	33-2[3]	46-11
		#2	29-10	43-9	33-2[3]	46-11
Hem-Fir	3/12	Sel. Str.	28-10	42-9	40-10[3]	42-9[2]
		#1	26-8	39-4	31-7	42-9[2]
		#2	25-6	37-6	27-11	39-2
	4/12	Sel. Str.	32-2	47-6	40-10[3]	47-6[2]
		#1	29-8	43-8	35-6[3]	47-6[2]
		#2	28-4	41-7	32-3	45-7
	5/12	Sel. Str.	33-8	49-6	40-10[3]	49-6[2]
		#1	30-11	45-5	35-6[3]	49-6[2]
		#2	29-6	43-3	32-5[3]	46-9[3]

see notes at end of Table G.4-b

TABLE G.2-b
Representative Roof Truss Spans for Selected Howe Trusses
for 610 mm on-center spacing with a total design load of 1915 pa
and a load duration increase of 15 percent (meters)

			TOP CHORD		BOTTOM CHORD	
			2x4	2x6	2x4	2x6
Southern Pine	3/12	#1 Dense	8.99	13.34	11.53	13.34^2
		#1	8.76	13.03	11.05	13.34^2
		#2 Dense	8.63	12.78	9.83	13.34^2
		#2	8.33	12.27	9.27	13.06
	4/12	#1 Dense	10.01	14.81	12.93	14.81^2
		#1	9.75	14.45	12.42^3	14.81^2
		#2 Dense	9.60	14.15	11.35	14.81^2
		#2	9.24	13.59	10.69	14.81^2
	5/12	#1 Dense	10.44	15.42	12.93^3	15.42^2
		#1	10.16	15.06	12.42^3	15.42^2
		#2 Dense	10.01	14.73	12.09^3	15.42^2
		#2	9.65	14.12	11.25^3	15.42^2
Douglas Fir-Larch	3/12	Sel. Str.	9.19	13.64	13.41^3	13.64^2
		#1 & Better	8.71	12.95	11.35	13.64^2
		#1	8.43	12.47	10.26	13.64^2
		#2	8.08	11.94	9.27	13.00
	4/12	Sel. Str.	10.24	15.14	13.41^3	15.14^2
		#1 & Better	9.70	14.35	12.34^3	15.14^2
		#1	9.35	13.82	11.40^3	15.14^2
		#2	8.97	13.23	10.31^3	14.91
	5/12	Sel. Str.	10.69	15.77	13.41^3	15.77^2
		#1 & Better	10.13	14.96	12.34^3	15.77^2
		#1	9.75	14.38	11.40^3	15.77^2
		#2	9.35	13.74	10.31^3	15.65^3
Spruce-Pine-Fir	3/12	Sel. Str.	8.51	15.60	10.82	12.60^2
		#1	7.80	11.51	7.85	10.82
		#2	7.80	11.51	7.85	10.82
	4/12	Sel. Str.	9.47	14.00	11.86^3	14.00^2
		#1	8.69	12.80	9.19	12.80
		#2	8.69	12.80	9.19	12.80
	5/12	Sel. Str.	9.91	14.61	11.86^3	14.61^2
		#1	9.09	13.34	10.11^3	14.30
		#2	9.09	13.34	10.11^3	14.30
Hem-Fir	3/12	Sel. Str.	8.79	13.03	12.45^3	13.03^2
		#1	8.13	11.99	9.63	13.03^2
		#2	7.77	11.43	8.51	11.94
	4/12	Sel. Str.	9.80	14.48	12.45^3	14.48^2
		#1	9.04	13.31	10.82^3	14.48^2
		#2	8.64	12.67	9.83	13.89
	5/12	Sel. Str.	10.26	15.09	12.45^3	15.09^2
		#1	9.42	13.84	10.82^3	15.09^2
		#2	8.99	13.18	9.88^3	14.25^3

see notes at end of Table G.4-b

TABLE G.3-a
Representative Roof Truss Spans for Selected Scissors Trusses
for 24-inch on-center spacing with a total design load of 40 psf
and a load duration increase of 15 percent (feet-inches)

			TOP CHORD		BOTTOM CHORD	
			2x4	2x6	2x4	2x6
Southern Pine	T.C. 3/12 B.C. 1.5/12	#1 Dense	21-9	32-5	24-6	32-5[2]
		#1	21-2	31-7	23-6	32-5[2]
		#2 Dense	20-11	31-2	20-2	28-6
		#2	20-1	29-11	19-0	26-8
	T.C. 4/12 B.C. 2/12	#1 Dense	24-2	35-11	29-9	35-11[2]
		#1	23-6	35-1	28-5	35-11[2]
		#2 Dense	23-3	34-6	24-9	35-2
		#2	22-5	33-2	23-5	32-10
	T.C. 5/12 B.C. 2.5/12	#1 Dense	25-11	38-7	33-10	38-7[2]
		#1	25-3	37-8	32-5	38-7[2]
		#2 Dense	25-0	37-0	28-6	38-7[2]
		#2	24-1	35-7	26-11	37-11
Douglas Fir-Larch	T.C. 3/12 B.C. 1.5/12	Sel. Str.	22-1	33-1	30-11	33-1[2]
		#1 & Better	21-0	31-5	24-10	33-1[2]
		#1	20-4	30-5	22-0	30-10
		#2	19-6	29-0	19-7	27-1
	T.C. 4/12 B.C. 2/12	Sel. Str.	24-7	36-8	36-6	36-8[2]
		#1 & Better	23-5	34-11	29-9	36-8[2]
		#1	22-8	33-9	26-8	36-8[2]
		#2	21-9	32-3	23-10	33-2
	T.C. 5/12 B.C. 2.5/12	Sel. Str.	26-6	39-5	39-3	39-5[2]
		#1 & Better	25-2	37-6	33-7	39-5[2]
		#1	24-5	36-3	30-2	39-5[2]
		#2	23-5	34-8	27-2	37-11
Spruce-Pine-Fir	T.C. 3/12 B.C. 1.5/12	Sel. Str.	20-4	30-5	22-8	30-5[2]
		#1	18-7	27-7	15-6	21-3
		#2	18-7	27-7	15-6	21-3
	T.C. 4/12 B.C. 2/12	Sel. Str.	22-9	33-10	27-7	33-10[2]
		#1	20-10	30-10	19-4	26-4
		#2	20-10	30-10	19-4	26-4
	T.C. 5/12 B.C. 2.5/12	Sel. Str.	24-6	36-4	31-7	36-4[2]
		#1	22-6	33-3	22-5	30-10
		#2	22-6	33-3	22-5	30-10
Hem-Fir	T.C. 3/12 B.C. 1.5/12	Sel. Str.	21-1	31-5	28-8	31-5[2]
		#1	19-6	29-1	20-3	28-0
		#2	18-8	27-9	17-5	24-2
	T.C. 4/12 B.C. 2/12	Sel. Str.	23-6	34-11	34-1	34-11[2]
		#1	21-10	32-4	24-8	34-5
		#2	20-10	30-10	21-5	29-10
	T.C. 5/12 B.C. 2.5/12	Sel. Str.	25-4	37-6	37-4	37-6[2]
		#1	23-6	34-9	28-2	37-6[2]
		#2	22-5	33-1	24-7	34-6

see notes at end of Table G.4-b

TABLE G.3-b
Representative Roof Truss Spans for Selected Scissors Trusses
for 610 mm on-center spacing with a total design load of 1915 pa
and a load duration increase of 15 percent (meters)

			TOP CHORD		BOTTOM CHORD	
			2x4	2x6	2x4	2x6
Southern Pine	T.C. 3/12 B.C. 1.5/12	#1 Dense	6.63	9.88	7.47	9.88[2]
		#1	6.45	9.63	7.16	9.88[2]
		#2 Dense	6.38	9.50	6.15	8.69
		#2	6.12	9.12	5.79	8.13
	T.C. 4/12 B.C. 2/12	#1 Dense	7.37	10.95	9.07	10.95[2]
		#1	7.16	10.69	8.66	10.95[2]
		#2 Dense	7.09	10.52	7.54	10.72
		#2	6.83	10.11	7.14	10.01
	T.C. 5/12 B.C. 2.5/12	#1 Dense	7.90	11.76	10.31	11.76[2]
		#1	7.70	11.48	9.88	11.76[2]
		#2 Dense	7.62	11.28	8.69	11.76[2]
		#2	7.34	10.85	8.20	11.56
Douglas Fir-Larch	T.C. 3/12 B.C. 1.5/12	Sel. Str.	6.73	10.08	9.42	10.08[2]
		#1 & Better	6.40	9.58	7.57	10.08[2]
		#1	6.20	9.27	6.71	9.40
		#2	5.94	8.84	5.97	8.25
	T.C. 4/12 B.C. 2/12	Sel. Str.	7.49	11.18	11.13	11.18[2]
		#1 & Better	7.14	10.64	9.07	11.18[2]
		#1	6.91	10.29	8.13	11.18[2]
		#2	6.63	9.83	7.26	10.11
	T.C. 5/12 B.C. 2.5/12	Sel. Str.	8.08	12.01	11.96	12.01[2]
		#1 & Better	7.67	11.43	10.24	12.01[2]
		#1	7.44	11.05	9.19	12.01[2]
		#2	7.14	10.57	8.28	11.56
Spruce-Pine-Fir	T.C. 3/12 B.C. 1.5/12	Sel. Str.	6.20	9.27	6.91	9.27[2]
		#1	5.66	8.41	4.72	6.48
		#2	5.66	8.41	4.72	6.48
	T.C. 4/12 B.C. 2/12	Sel. Str.	6.93	10.31	8.41	10.31[2]
		#1	6.35	10.31	5.89	8.03
		#2	6.35	10.31	5.89	8.03
	T.C. 5/12 B.C. 2.5/12	Sel. Str.	7.47	11.07	9.63	11.07[2]
		#1	6.86	10.13	6.83	9.40
		#2	6.86	10.13	6.83	9.40
Hem-Fir	T.C. 3/12 B.C. 1.5/12	Sel. Str.	6.43	9.58	8.74	9.58[2]
		#1	5.94	8.86	6.17	8.53
		#2	5.69	8.46	5.31	7.37
	T.C. 4/12 B.C. 2/12	Sel. Str.	7.16	10.64	10.39	10.64[2]
		#1	6.65	9.86	7.52	10.49
		#2	6.65	9.40	6.53	9.09
	T.C. 5/12 B.C. 2.5/12	Sel. Str.	7.72	11.43	11.38	11.43[2]
		#1	7.16	10.59	8.59	11.43[2]
		#2	6.83	10.08	7.49	10.51

see notes at end of Table G.4-b

TABLE G.4-a
Representative Roof Truss Spans for Selected King Post Trusses
for 24-inch on-center spacing with a total design load of 40 psf
and a load duration increase of 15 percent (feet-inches)

			TOP CHORD		BOTTOM CHORD	
			2x4	2x6	2x4	2x6
Southern Pine	3/12	#1 Dense	17-2	25-1	21-6[3]	25-1[2]
		#1	16-9	24-7	20-8[3]	25-1[2]
		#2 Dense	16-4	23-9	20-1[3]	25-1[2]
		#2	15-8	22-7	18-9[3]	25-1[2]
	4/12	#1 Dense	17-10	26-0	21-6[3]	26-0[2]
		#1	17-4	25-5	20-8[3]	26-0[2]
		#2 Dense	16-11	24-6	20-1[3]	26-0[2]
		#2	16-2	23-3	18-9[3]	26-0[2]
	5/12	#1 Dense	18-2	26-7	21-6[3]	26-7[2]
		#1	17-8	25-11	20-8[3]	26-7[2]
		#2 Dense	17-3	25-0	20-1[3]	26-7[2]
		#2	16-6	23-8	18-9[3]	26-3[3]
Douglas Fir-Larch	3/12	Sel. Str.	17-8	25-10	22-4[3]	25-10[2]
		#1 & Better	16-6	24-2	20-7[3]	25-10[2]
		#1	15-9	23-0	19-0[3]	25-10[2]
		#2	15-0	21-10	17-3[3]	25-10[2]
	4/12	Sel. Str.	18-4	26-9	22-4[3]	26-9[2]
		#1 & Better	17-1	24-11	20-7[3]	26-9[2]
		#1	16-3	23-8	19-0[3]	26-9[2]
		#2	15-5	22-5	17-3[3]	26-0[3]
	5/12	Sel. Str.	18-9	27-4	22-4[3]	27-4[2]
		#1 & Better	17-5	25-4	20-7[3]	27-4[2]
		#1	16-7	24-1	19-0[3]	27-0[3]
		#2	15-8	22-10	17-3[3]	26-0[3]
Spruce-Pine-Fir	3/12	Sel. Str.	16-5	24-0	19-9[3]	24-0[2]
		#1	14-9	21-5	16-10[3]	24-0[2]
		#2	14-9	21-5	16-10[3]	24-0[2]
	4/12	Sel. Str.	17-1	24-10	19-9[3]	24-10[2]
		#1	15-3	22-1	16-10[3]	24-6[3]
		#2	15-3	22-1	16-10[3]	24-6[3]
	5/12	Sel. Str.	17-6	25-5	19-9[3]	25-5[2]
		#1	15-6	22-6	16-10[3]	24-6[3]
		#2	15-6	22-6	16-10[3]	24-6[3]
Hem-Fir	3/12	Sel. Str.	17-1	24-11	20-8[3]	24-11[2]
		#1	15-4	22-3	18-1[3]	24-11[2]
		#2	14-7	21-2	16-6[3]	23-8[3]
	4/12	Sel. Str.	17-10	25-11	20-8[3]	25-11[2]
		#1	15-10	22-11	18-1[3]	25-5[3]
		#2	15-1	21-10	16-6[3]	23-8[3]
	5/12	Sel. Str.	18-3	26-6	20-8[3]	26-6[2]
		#1	16-1	23-4	18-1[3]	25-5[3]
		#2	15-4	22-2	16-6[3]	23-8[3]

see notes at end of Table G.4-b

TABLE G.4-b
Representative Roof Truss Spans for Selected King Post Trusses
for 610 mm on-center spacing with a total design load of 1915 pa
and a load duration increase of 15 percent (meters)

			TOP CHORD		BOTTOM CHORD	
			2x4	2x6	2x4	2x6
Southern Pine	3/12	#1 Dense	5.23	7.65	6.55^3	7.65^2
		#1	5.11	7.49	6.30^3	7.65^2
		#2 Dense	4.98	7.24	6.12^3	7.65^2
		#2	4.78	6.88	5.72^3	7.65^2
	4/12	#1 Dense	5.44	7.92	6.55^3	7.92^2
		#1	5.28	7.75	6.30^3	7.92^2
		#2 Dense	5.16	7.47	6.12^3	7.92^2
		#2	4.93	7.09	5.72^3	7.92^2
	5/12	#1 Dense	5.54	8.10	6.55^3	8.10^2
		#1	5.38	7.90	6.30^3	8.10^2
		#2 Dense	5.26	7.62	6.12^3	8.10^2
		#2	5.03	7.21	5.72^3	8.00^3
Douglas Fir-Larch	3/12	Sel. Str.	5.38	7.87	6.81^3	7.87^2
		#1 & Better	5.03	7.37	6.27^3	7.87^2
		#1	4.80	7.01	5.79^3	7.87^2
		#2	4.57	6.65	5.26^3	7.87^2
	4/12	Sel. Str.	5.59	8.15	6.81^3	8.15^2
		#1 & Better	5.21	7.59	6.27^3	8.15^2
		#1	4.95	7.21	5.79^3	8.15^2
		#2	4.70	6.83	5.26^3	7.92^3
	5/12	Sel. Str.	5.72	8.33	6.81^3	8.33^2
		#1 & Better	5.31	7.72	6.27^3	8.33^2
		#1	5.05	7.34	5.79^3	8.23^3
		#2	4.78	6.96	5.26^3	7.92^3
Spruce-Pine-Fir	3/12	Sel. Str.	5.00	7.32	6.02^3	7.32^2
		#1	4.50	6.53	5.13^3	7.32^2
		#2	4.50	6.53	5.13^3	7.32^2
	4/12	Sel. Str.	5.21	7.57	6.02^3	7.57^2
		#1	4.65	6.73	5.13^3	7.47^3
		#2	4.65	6.73	5.13^3	7.47^3
	5/12	Sel. Str.	5.33	7.75	6.02^3	7.75^2
		#1	4.72	6.86	5.13^3	6.86^3
		#2	4.72	6.86	5.13^3	6.86^3
Hem-Fir	3/12	Sel. Str.	5.21	7.59	6.30^3	7.59^2
		#1	4.67	6.78	5.51^3	7.59^2
		#2	4.44	6.45	5.03^3	7.21^3
	4/12	Sel. Str.	5.44	7.90	6.30^3	7.90^2
		#1	4.83	6.99	5.51^3	7.75^3
		#2	4.60	6.65	5.03^3	7.21^3
	5/12	Sel. Str.	5.56	8.08	6.30^3	8.08^2
		#1	4.90	7.11	5.51^3	7.75^3
		#2	4.67	6.76	5.03^3	7.21^3

Design Criteria: Top Chord Live Load   = 20 psf (958 Pa)
                          Top Chord Dead Load   = 10 psf (479 Pa)
                          Bottom Chord Live Load = 0 psf   (0 Pa)
                          Bottom Chord Dead Load = 10 psf (479 Pa)

Notes: Truss spans shown above are examples of truss spans for the loadings and truss configurations shown. The tables are not intended to be used for design purposes or specific projects.

Spans have been determined in accordance with the design Specifications for Metal Plate Connected Wood Trusses, TPI-92, of the Truss Plate Institute (TPI) and the 1991 edition of the National Design Specification for Wood Construction (NDS®) of the American Forest and Paper Association (AFPA).
Tables shown are not intended to limit roof trusses to these loads, lumber species, grades, and configurations. See your WTCA member fabricator for actual truss designs and solutions to custom roof profiles. Some representative spans for the configurations shown may vary with each fabricator.

Footnotes: 1.   Representative spans shown assume that the moisture content of the lumber does not exceed 19% at time of fabrication and during end use.

                2.   Representative span for this lumber grade has been limited to the representative truss span that can be achieved by the group of lumber grades provided in these tables.

                3.   Representative span for this lumber grade has been limited by the representative bottom chord panel length based on the TPI requirement of applying 200 lb. (890 N) concentrated load to represent a construction worker standing on the bottom chord.

Ref: *Metal Plate Connected Wood Truss Handbook.* Wood Truss Council of America, Madison, WI. 1993. Used by permission of WTCA.